# NEW PLAINS REVIEW

I0553754

## Fall 2015

### Editors and Staff

| | |
|---|---|
| Executive Editor | Shay Rahm |
| Production Chief | Michelle Lee Waggoner |
| Editor-in-Chief | Brendon Yuill |
| Managing Editor | Pati Hailey |
| Poetry Editor | Mary Inselman |
| Assistant Poetry Editors | Josh Grizzly Shepard |
| | Joshua Barnett |
| Fiction Editor | Jessie Layfield |
| Assistant Fiction Editors | Madison Castelli |
| | Ashley Hoffmeier |
| | Treyce Glidden |
| | Alicia Plotz |
| Non-fiction Editor | Anna Hester |
| Assistant Non-fiction Editor | Megan Biedermann |
| Social Media Manager | Alicia Plotz |
| | Josh Grizzly Shepard |
| Webmaster | William Andrews |

New Plains Review Publishing Group
University of Central Oklahoma
Edmond, Oklahoma

NEW PLAINS REVIEW

ISBN-10: 0-9837357-8-6
ISBN-13: 978-0-9837357-8-6

*New Plains Review* is a literary journal published
each academic semester, sponsored by the English
Department, College of Liberal Arts, at the University
of Central Oklahoma. The image found on every cover
of *New Plains Review* issue since 2000 is based on a
painting titled "Phantom Warriors" by acclaimed Native
American artist and UCO alumnus Sherman Chaddlesone.

*New Plains Review*
English Department, Box 184
University of Central Oklahoma
100 North University Drive
Edmond, Oklahoma 73034
(405) 974-5613

newplainsreview@gmail.com
www.libarts.uco.edu/english/newplains

Submission Information: *New Plains Review*
accepts original work in prose, poetry, drama, fiction, art,
and photography. Submissions are accepted by email. For
editorial guidelines, please visit the website.

Ordering Information: Pricing for subscriptions,
current and back issues are available through the website.

IMAGE CREDITS

Cover Illustration
*Michelle Waggoner*

Section Feature Art
*Ariana Foote*

# Foreword

*Imagination, not intelligence, made us human.*
                                                – Terry Pratchett

For each edition of the *New Plains Review*, we receive countless submissions from writers and artists all across the world. And with each edition, we are never disappointed with the total mastery of imagination, creativity, and craftsmanship that we witness from what we receive.

The freedom to display creativity and self-expression has always been of the utmost importance to the *New Plains Review* as a literary journal. All of the pieces that we have chosen — from "Elmo in the Passenger Seat" to "When Bouncing Bettys and Truth Collide" — are works that we feel promote this idea of creativity both in narrative and in style exceptionally, allowing our readers to continue to view the world in ways that they may not have considered before — in a way that only art and literature can provide.

We are proud of the imagination and creativity of the artists and writers whose works we have displayed in this journal, and we are pleased to present to you the Fall 2015 Edition of the *New Plains Review*.

Brendon Yuill
Editor-in-Chief

# Contents

**POETRY**

Daily Life
*Taehyun Han* ............................................................................ 9

After Hours
*Paul Bernstein* ......................................................................... 10

Asking for Sugar
*Sam Herschel Wein* .................................................................. 11

Birds, Waking
*Steve Nickman* ......................................................................... 12

After Surgery
*Amie Sharp* .............................................................................. 13

For the Holdouts
*Amie Sharp* .............................................................................. 14

Eighteen Confessions
*Addison Eaton* .......................................................................... 16

How Brave They Were
*Mark Burke* .............................................................................. 18

When You Were Born
*Mark Burke* .............................................................................. 20

Housewife
*Jon Ballard* .............................................................................. 22

Perspective
*Neelanjana Shakya* ................................................................... 23

Spring Cleaning
*Kaycee Chance* .......................................................................... 24

Lessons From a Crow
*Kaycee Chance* .......................................................................... 26

The Fall of Man
*Michael Constantine McConnell* ............................................... 27

The River is Wide
*Seth Benton* .............................................................................. 28

**VISUAL ART**

Most Efficient Hunter
*Jessica Scott* .............................................................................. 33

chRch
*Joshua Garrett* .......................................................................... 34

WR PRTY
*Joshua Garrett* .......................................................................... 35

Sam
*Scott Reno* ................................................................................ 36

Summer Dreams
*Scott Reno* ................................................................................ 37

Self Attack: The Ride
*Allen Forrest* ........................................................... 38
Sunset Reflections
*Una Belle Townsend* ................................................. 39
Repetitive Direction
*Elizabeth Brown* ..................................................... 40
Convoluted Movement
*Elizabeth Brown* ..................................................... 41
Gift to the Packers Future 2013 First Round Draft Pick (Datone Jones)
*Michael Litzau* ...................................................... 42
Untitled (beauties)
*Ariana Foote* ........................................................ 43

## FICTION

Antonio
*Michael Cuglietta* .................................................. 47
Dean Amuck
*Gary A. Berg* ....................................................... 53
Caryatid
*Kirie C. Pedersen* .................................................. 63
Too Big to Carry
*Tara Isabel Zambrano* .............................................. 77
EDITORS' PRIZE: Elmo in the Passenger Seat
*Michael P. Adams* ................................................. 79

## NON-FICTION

Blown Away: Paul B. Sears and Oklahoma
*Michael Snyder* .................................................... 89
When Bouncing Bettys and Truth Collide
*Brenden Stovall* .................................................... 93
Squirrel on the Roof
*Francis DiClemente* ................................................ 99

## ABOUT THE
## CONTRIBUTORS

Poetry ................................................................. 105
Visual Art ............................................................. 108
Fiction ................................................................ 111
Non-fiction ........................................................... 112

# POETRY

# Daily Life

*Taehyun Han*

*fear eats soul*

It hides in the shadow of late afternoon
It slithers its way behind my back
and coils up in my soft heart

Despite the summer sun high in the sky,
a chill grips my stomach like a swallow of ice

When the shrill of cicadas dies down
and every wall, every ceiling,
roaches and spiders stop to listen in my misery,

It bursts out of my heart
and laughs, sitting on my carcass until its mouth splits

# After Hours

*Paul Bernstein*

Seared by the thick
red silence of sunsets,
I, stick-shape,
driven by jukeboxes,
sit beside somebody
else's woman, bonded
by the electric
communion of guitars.
The singer's eyes
are shut, one hand
cupped behind an ear
to catch the pitch; his
voice explodes, stomp
and rhythm of the beat
jolts us into whirling,
transitory union.
The music ends;
silence shoos us back
into our separate space,
nothing left to do
but leave.

# Asking for Sugar

*Sam Herschel Wein*

Pink grapefruits,
preciously sweet, a sharp-
edged spoon that is pressure
beyond what the skin can
take; *I wanna fuck you
so bad* he snarls behind my
gums, his mind a pink
pasty flower gritted
to no petals at
all, my mind a pain like
bitter coffee or consuming
cigarettes whole to see
if nicotine works in the stomach
too. It didn't. I didn't
teeth his white lace seeds,
didn't squeeze any skin 'til juice
dropped in the bowl,
I didn't ask for sugar or spit or
anything
smooth to guide the taste
down something small, sour
stinging on every nerve, vitamins
lost like
my body is
supposed to swallow everything
whole. At breakfast, I can't
eat the fruit out the too-
white bowl, a pink so plush
its palpable and pain-
ridden passed, *take it you
little pussy* a mantra for fruits
and breakfast fruits
and cigarettes that don't
taste like smoke anymore
that don't taste like
I can eat anymore.

# Birds, Waking

*Steve Nickman*

My Carolina wren
breaches gray, still air:
I see you, I see you!
but then recants:
No voyeur, no voyeur.

Robin, ontologist,
in search of God pursues
the "credo quia absurdum,"
asks himself, then answers:
Is it? Is it? It is! It is!

Crow is a grating syllable
but what a motormouth the jay!
One prolix, one succinct,
with raucous authority
each claims the day.

The mocker apes their songs —
an idiot-savant —
dons Cardinal's carmine robe.
His Eminence arrives and patiently
corrects his Latin consonants.

Mourning dove, awakened late,
proclaims love's disillusionment.
He chants his woe, but then she's there
beside him on the branch. Abashed
he murmurs, no lament.

Captive of symphony —
chipping sparrow's one-note offering
is Shostakovich in his Fifth,
ends his first movement with a bell,
just Ting!

# After Surgery

*Amie Sharp*


A breath like the other side
        of birth, fluorescent bulbs
humming the hospital air.
          Metal blips cutting the distance

of sleep, the bulk of anesthesia,
        what started as an antiseptic
cloud spiriting me into a Hadean
        stupor I'd grown to love.

Ceiling tiles blazing yellow,
        harsh with nausea.
The blue-dotted gown hypnotic,
        halls dizzying with the Vertigo

effect as attendants zoomed me
        from floor to floor,
the worst theme park ride ever:
        Pirates of the Outpatient Ward.

The sutures' first current of throb
        and prickle, my abdomen
bubbled with stitched glue.
        My hair frazzling like Einstein's

under my husband's washcloth.
        And then, linoleum and mirrors
sparking me into a marvelous uncoiling
        now: this wheelchair's soft whine

ushering me through electric doors.
        This nurse's kind prattle.
These solid arms I love so much
        lifting me into the car

to take me home. This December wind
        smacking me with its cold
delicious sting. This night air
        teeming with gossamer snow.

# For the Holdouts

*Amie Sharp*

In China, they call them "nail houses."
In Seattle, Edith Macefield
declined a million dollars
for her $120,000 home,
steadfast as the concrete
honeycombed around her,
a crane whomping
its weight into steel supports,
the jackhammering so loud
it must have numbed
into something like silence
inside the segmented rooms
with their green upholstery,
their houseplants and picture frames.

Her right to refuse
meant staying in a narrow plot,
the only one surrounded
not by neighbors
but buildings with skylights
that will one day cloud,
and concrete floor-slabs
hived with shoppers —
a Trader Joe's on one side,
LA Fitness on the other.

She'd filled the house
with books and stacks of letters —
some from her cousin,
Benny Goodman. She'd played clarinet
with the Dorseys and written
a thousand page novel
called *Where Yesterday Began.*
And when it was all over she left
the little house to the construction
superintendent who'd become
her last friend.

Is this the heart of defiance —
saying no when it holds back nothing
in the lit black of night?
From outside, in the fluorescence
of the signs flamed around
the boarded house, who can say?
Maybe she would say
it was never about rebellion,
never about money,
and never about what
would happen after she was gone.
Maybe it was only that she made
her home where she wanted
while she was here.

# Eighteen Confessions

*Addison Eaton*

A nurse in faded green scrubs asks me my name.
I tell her my name is Stardust.
I tell her my name is Demise.
She writes it down in hastened chicken scratch,
making my existence look so fragile,
so meager.

"Age?"
"Eighteen," I whisper.
I am eighteen,
but I feel so much older.

I am eighteen lines of ancient text.
I am seventeen shards of glass at the end of an ancient Roman soldier's
whip.
I am the sixteen streaks of crimson that run down the prisoner's mangled
back.
The blood that runs through my veins comes from
inventors,
artists,
and revolutionaries.
My DNA tells the story of those who broke rules,
who stood up against the tyrants of their day.

Fifteen times I loved.
Fourteen times I've lost.
I said yes to thirteen liars, beggars, and thieves.
Only I know the reason why.

My father stopped hugging me when I was twelve.
It took eleven seconds for the paramedics to revive me, or so they say.
And ten more minutes to regain consciousness.
Sometimes I wish I could regress back to birth;
a nine month break from reality.

I look at the woman who is doing my intake paperwork,
observing the crease in her eyebrows
and the hurried demeanor she wears like a timepiece.
To her I am merely a name on a page.
She knows nothing of my story.
Nor does she care.

What if I told her the angels came to me when I died?
What if I told her that demons were the true secret keepers,
and creation was eight days long.
Not seven.

The last day God cried.
Or drank.
I know I would.

There are six letters in my name
and I am so much more than five numbers on a hospital bracelet.
Yet with four clicks of her tongue, she's made up her mind.
Three more questions, and she's got a solid idea of who she thinks I am.

The clock chimes two.
I am one girl in a room full of ghosts.
I am primordial and ephemeral.
I am eighteen paradoxes stacked inward,
like a fucked up set of nesting dolls.

"Eighteen is too young to be here, young lady."
I smile.

# How Brave They Were

*Mark Burke*

After my father and mother
came home from work,
the three of us would go
to clean a small factory at night.
My father divided
the cavern of cubicles between us
and we separated
to empty the garbage, mop bathrooms,
a whining harmony of vacuums
droning through the castle.

I was seventeen
and never said as we worked
that I was drifting
from any faith in their god.
When the priest told them
there was nothing for me
at the church school,
they let me leave
when I wanted to go.

I wandered, waiting tables,
worked the winter in a sawmill,
moved west with spring.
I saw so many at night in the city parks
sleeping in the woods.
Each town was like a cubicle,
square and worn, a makeshift place.
I'd walk for days, camped in libraries,
Greyhound stations, trying to stay dry,
trying to unravel a confusion

without knowing what to call it.
They were Cape Breton islanders
who let me go without knowing where,
a prince and a saint who
offered what they could,
these two I talk to every day,
gone to what they believed.

Even now, a comfort comes
from a vacuum's pitched moan
whirring in the room beside mine.

# When You Were Born

*Mark Burke*

When your mother was carrying you
and the time was close,
I was working the night shift
at the American Motors plant,
a station on the paint line,
where for eight hours I scuffed out faults
in the prime-coat on the body's metal.
I stood as the constant droning
flow of hollow shells crept past me
on a wheeled conveyor.

For seventeen seconds I'd sand
as the car dragged slowly past,
then read for twenty
before the next body appeared.
I could get through a page of Roman history,
cover the book with a rag,
turn and sand, read then buff,
one after another after another.

In the middle of one night,
I thought I heard my name
slip across the din.
It sounded like my father
when I'd broken his rule again.
But he wasn't there and I read on
how Romans kept kitchen-spirit statues
and I thought we'd make ours out of clay,
kilned and glazed in blue oxide.

But the voice kept calling louder
until I saw the foreman
marching down the line and I froze,
caught again trying to keep
from drowning.
He shouted at me
to get to the hospital
you would soon be here.
I stood for a moment and stared
at the river of metal hulks rolling past,
imagining who you would be.

# Housewife

*Jon Ballard*

That kitchen devoured
mother, sopped her up
in butter and bacon fat.
Stool-high cupboards
that stuck, never bare,
but empty a way
only she could see.

One window over
the counter grimed
by greasy eons — pried
open for lilacs two
weeks in spring
every year, the only
perfume she wore.

# Perspective

*Neelanjana Shakya*

As I looked upon that purple space
I saw even more of it gather slowly
beneath the sundrop;
a single spectrum
slipped over the rainbow
and seduced the sky.

And as I sat there on the rock,
the waves rocking beneath my feet,
pulling in pigments,
gently pinking clear pearls
and purpling the sea;
the scene became a monochrome
staining my mind
and every other heartbeat.

# Spring Cleaning

*Kaycee Chance*

I open my eyes and sit up in bed.
It's early, but I've already resigned myself
To nothingness.
No hopes
No longing
No anger
Because there you'll be
In all of them.

My feet swing out from under the blankets
And touch the floor.
They are brittle,
Made up of every lie I've ever told,
And I am wearing at the soles.
The soft pitter patter of flesh on the floor
Is the sound of my apathy
Because I am not allowed to care
About you.
I was never allowed to care
About you.

I float around the house all day.
The ghost of myself. A shell.
An empty pack of cigarettes
When you just need one puff.
I catch a glimpse of myself in the mirror
And gasp. I can see how much
You've wasted me.

And I would gladly curl up
Inside every laugh line on your face,
Inside twenty-one years of you
That came before me.
But I never will again.
And I'm wondering if you miss
Waking up to blonde hair on your pillow.

I put on a record
That sounds like your laughter.

If I stop moving now,
I'll see your smile in my mind.
And just maybe,
I'll smile, too.
But god forbid that happens,
Because something that holy,
That sacred,
Doesn't belong to you anymore.

I set your memory on fire,
Your old shirts, notes on bar napkins,
Pictures of you
With that smile.
I burn it all in the same fireplace
We once sat in front of
Drinking
Laughing
Hurting
Melting.
I shake you out of the sheets on my bed,
And in the sunlight I see you in the dust.

All of you disposed,
Just as easily as you did of me.

# Lessons From a Crow

*Kaycee Chance*

I saw a bird in summer's rain alive
In warmth and light. The perch was bare; the leaves
Were gone. But there he sat, not caring he
Was alone. He saw darker clouds across
The pond, another storm was rolling North.
He bent his head under his wing, in wait
For storms to come. I like to think someday
That I could weather life so well. But where
To tuck my heart or head? I ask, but he
Sits still, perhaps not knowing what to say.
I'll ask him again tomorrow, but I
Do need to know today. "Hello?" I beg,
"I have no wings to shield myself from storms
Or life, or love." He flies to me and lands
Upon my window sill and sings to me
*A song so sad, he knows my wounds are deep.*
*In life we learn to take shelter, but now*
*We must begin to teach ourselves to stand*
*Inside the eye of life's big storms under*
*The darkest skies. The rain won't stop because*
*Of you, and life won't even pause for you.*
I saw a bird in summer's rain, alive …

# The Fall of Man

*Michael Constantine McConnell*

As we held hands at church and hummed
the oldest song in the world, I
never asked about lightning's gender,

only wanted to spend the rest
of my life blinking back at you.
You were the one I wanted

to prove the world wrong with,
and I turned into yolk in your arms,
where the cost of loving was too great.

Winged cellular forms gave the spiders
whisky and measured bird-beaked
resentment one shot glass at a time.

When you praised God that you'd left me,
I had to forgive Hell itself
and apologize for being,

impressed, embrace the terminal
disease of false humility.
Too many men had emptied you.

I still waited through each morning,
smoking cigarettes alone,
knowing you'd never come back.

# The River is Wide

*Seth Benton*

*New Year's Day*

Turkey vultures in a slow swirl
gathering down this side
of the river, marking a death.
On a narrow strip of beach
where an unnamed creek
splits a marsh
feeding into the river,
a doe lies fixed in relief,
her fur a shade darker
than the sand she rests on,
eyes gouged,
white leather of skin
rims the breach
in her belly.
A few winter flies
scavenge her ribs,
just the legs unchanged
as if refusing the heaviness
of death they could rise
to cross the winter marsh again.

*January 15*

Ice clings in the crevices
along the river's torn edges.
A wrack line of beach
grasses at the border of marsh
marks a temporary path.
The doe is there,
the stripped hull of her
ribs anchored in sand,
her life transferred
to bird, insect, fish.
What remains is unwanted;
the earth will receive it.
The river is a mile wide,
formed by two rivers
to the west converging,
energy feeding energy,
water carrying water to the sea.

# VISUAL ART

# Most Efficient Hunter

*Jessica Scott*

# chRch

*Joshua Garrett*

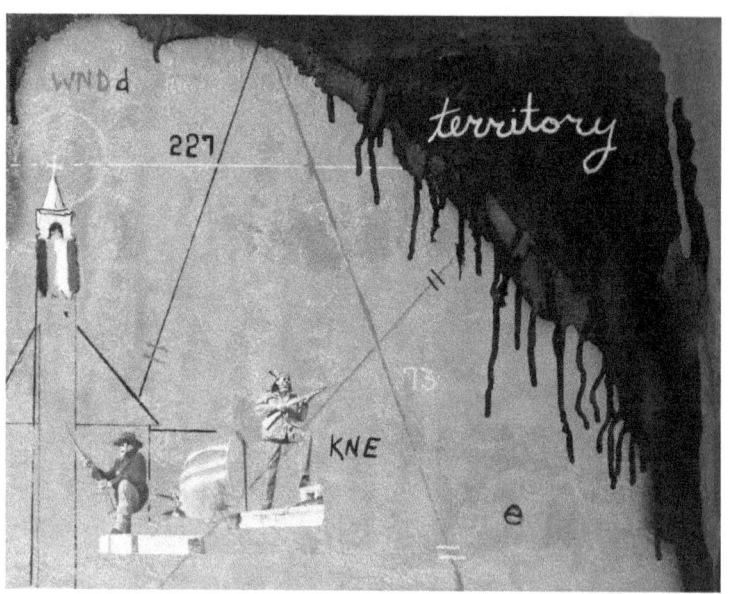

# WR PRTY

*Joshua Garrett*

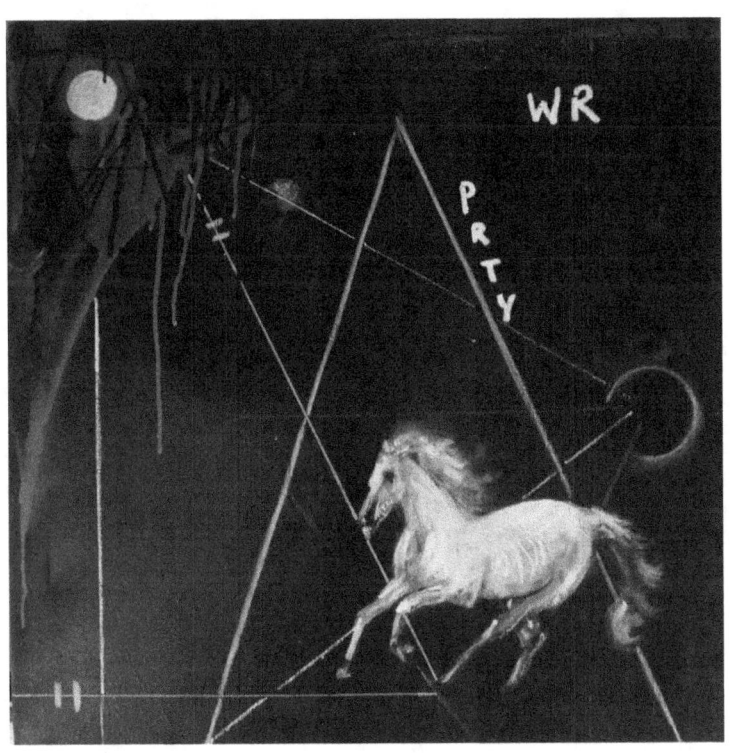

# Sam

*Scott Reno*

# Summer Dreams

*Scott Reno*

# Self Attack: The Ride

*Allen Forrest*

# Sunset Reflections

*Una Belle Townsend*

# Repetitive Direction

*Elizabeth Brown*

5 ½"H x 10"W x 6"D, 2009, paper, graphite

# Convoluted Movement

*Elizabeth Brown*

10' D, foam, plaster, dye, acrylic

# Gift to the Packers
# Future 2013 First Round Draft Pick
# (Datone Jones)

*Michael Litzau*

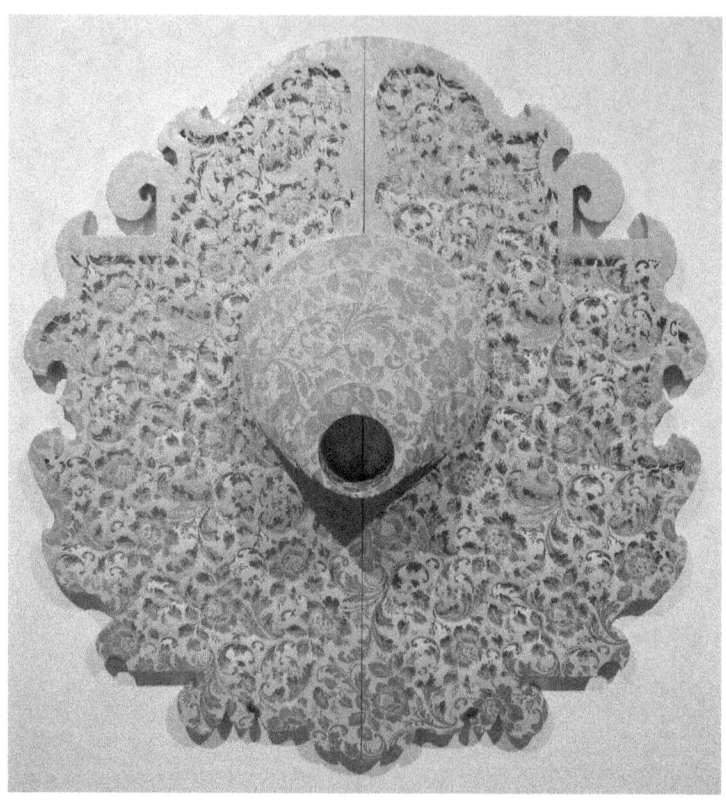

40"w x 40"h x 9"d, 2013, hand cut wall paper

# Untitled (beauties)

*Ariana Foote*

36"w x 80"h, ink and acrylic on mylar

# FICTION

# Antonio

## *Michael Cuglietta*

Antonio walked into the supermarket wearing a baggy sweatshirt with a large pocket in front. Inside the pocket, with both hands, he gripped a .38 caliber revolver.

There was a display of beach balls by the entrance. A little blonde girl was chasing her brother, trying to tag him with one of the inflatable balls. She ran with her head down, not paying attention to where she was going. She collided with Antonio, hitting him with enough force to knock her to the ground.

Antonio took his hands out of his pocket and helped the girl to her feet. There was no sound in the black and white footage, but I could tell the girl was crying. Her mother came rushing over and scooped her up into her arms. With a smile, Antonio ruffled her hair then, putting his hands back in his pocket, headed towards the back of the store.

The supermarket turned the security footage over to the police. Once the investigation was finished, it was deemed public domain, and *The Orlando Sentinel* posted it on their website.

I clicked the pause button and watched as Antonio's face froze on my computer screen. It had been a few months since I'd last seen him. He'd put on a lot of weight.

I wasn't sure I should continue watching. I thought of the beheading video that came out during the Iraq War. I wished I'd never seen it. It was the type of thing that, once you saw it, you couldn't put it out of your mind, no matter how hard you tried.

I closed the laptop and put it on my nightstand. It was 5AM, two hours before I had to be up for work. I turned my alarm off and opened the window, sending a rush of cold air into the room. I leaned out and, in the street, saw Jessica's car. Her front bumper was up on the curb. She'd missed the mailbox by mere inches.

I put on a pair of flannel pants then went into the kitchen. I ground some coffee beans and put them in the French press. Then, I filled the kettle with tap water and set it on the stove.

I could see a light coming from the guest room. I held my ear to the door and heard the television. Gently, I knocked. When I got no answer, I pushed the door open.

Jessica was asleep on the air mattress. Next to her, she had a suitcase, which, over the last couple of weeks, had served as both her dresser and her end table. On top, she had her cell phone and a mostly empty bottle of red wine.

In her sleep, she'd kicked the covers to the floor. She was wearing a thin white t-shirt that stopped an inch above her bellybutton and white cotton underwear that showed most of her ass. I touched her bare feet. They were like ice. I backed out of the room, leaving the covers on the floor.

I went to the bathroom and, inside the medicine cabinet, found a box of nicotine gum. I stuffed three pieces in my mouth and sat down on the toilet. Yesterday's paper was laying on the bathmat. They'd printed a picture of Antonio and his wife, Josephine. It took up half the front page. They were standing in front of a Christmas tree, their arms around each other. Antonio was wearing a red sweater. Josephine was in a tight green dress. Both had Santa hats on their heads.

On the inside of the paper, there was a picture of Josephine in her work uniform. After leaving Antonio, she got a job at the grocery store. In just a few short months, she'd been promoted from bagger to cashier.

As often as he used to talk about his wife, Antonio never told me she was so much younger than him. The article said the police had been out to their house three times in the last year, answering domestic disturbance calls. Each time, Josephine had refused to press charges. She was only allowed in the country because her husband had citizenship. If he went to jail, she risked being sent back to the Philippines.

The kettle began to scream. I got off the toilet as fast as I could. But, by the time I made it to the kitchen, Jessica was already there.

"I didn't mean to wake you." I took the kettle off the stove and poured the water over the coffee grinds.

There was a basket of clean clothes sitting on the kitchen table. "I told you to stop doing my laundry." At the bottom of the basket, she found a pair of sweatpants. "Why's it so cold in here? You forget to pay the gas bill again?"

I watched as she stepped into the pants. Then, she found a bra and, without removing her shirt, clipped it on.

"I'm going to heat up some oatmeal. Would you like some?" I poured two cups of coffee, gave one to her and kept the other for myself.

"No. I don't want any oatmeal." She held the mug to her face, letting the steam wash over her. "You have to stop with this shit."

"Someone woke up on the wrong side of the bed."

"You mean the wrong side of the air mattress?" She went into the guest room and came back with her cigarettes and a book of matches.

I mixed the rest of the hot water with a packet of dry oatmeal and took it to the table with my coffee.

"Why are you up so early?" she said, sitting across from me.

"Couldn't sleep." I took one bite of the oatmeal, pushed it aside and reached for her cigarettes. She slapped my hand away.

"I thought you were quitting?"

"Just one?" Again, I reached for the box. "Please."

She put two cigarettes between her lips, lit them both with the same match and passed one to me. "How's everyone at the office?" she asked.

"Connors wants a counselor to come by."

"Counselor?" She walked over to the cabinet and got a mug. She set it on the table to use as an ashtray.

"A crisis counselor."

"Jesus. Is it that bad?" She let out a cloud of smoke.

"Everyone loved Antonio."

"Did you see the article in yesterday's paper?" She ate a spoonful of oatmeal and made a face. "The guy was a real lunatic."

"It's hard to believe. He seemed like such a nice guy." I reached for the oatmeal. "Want me to get some brown sugar? It's good with brown sugar."

"Sean, please." She punched her cigarette out. Then lit another. "The paper said he hired a private investigator to track her down. If a guy ever treated me like that, I'd wait for him to fall asleep, then I'd cut his balls off."

From the cupboard, I got a bag of brown sugar. I mixed some into the oatmeal. "Much better." I spoke with my mouth full.

"I'm going to take a shower." She got up, took her cigarettes, and went into the bathroom.

I waited until I heard the water and then went into the guest room. There was a green light on her phone, blinking with a message. There were two missed calls, both from the same number.

It wasn't hard to figure out her password. She always used either her birthday or our anniversary. I held the phone to my ear and heard a man's voice.

*Hey, Sweetheart, just calling to make sure you made it home. I don't know about you, but my head is throbbing. What were we thinking ordering that third bottle? Text me when you get this, let me know you made it home safe.*

I left the phone on the mattress, went into the bathroom, and sat on the toilet seat. The newspaper was still laying on the bathmat. Looking at the photograph, I couldn't wrap my mind around the age difference.

Josephine was beautiful, with big brown eyes and dark curly hair. Standing next to her, Antonio looked like Frankenstein. The paper talked about his struggles with alcohol. According to the reporter, he'd been in and out of Alcoholics Anonymous for decades. I never knew about his drinking. But I was well aware of his problems with pain pills. He'd gotten addicted after his back surgery. Some days he'd take so many, he'd nod off while on the phone with a client.

I was so focused on the paper I didn't notice Jessica had turned the shower off. She pulled the curtain aside and, seeing me, just about jumped through the ceiling.

"Jesus Christ." She held her hand over her chest. "Are you trying to give me a heart attack?" Realizing she was naked, she covered as much as she could with her hands. I got a towel and went to wrap it around her shoulders. She snatched it away from me.

"You shouldn't be in here," she said.

"I've seen you naked a million times."

"It's different now." She stepped out of the shower and stood in front of the mirror, rubbing lotion on her arms.

"All those nights you said you were working late. That was bullshit, wasn't it?" I tried to make eye contact in the mirror. "It's one of the doctors from work, isn't it?"

"Maybe you should hire Antonio's private investigator." She pushed me aside and put one foot on the toilet seat. She spread lotion on her leg, starting at the ankle and moving up towards her thigh.

"I don't want to fight," she said, finishing with the first leg and moving to the next. "You should know, I'm getting my own place." She had the towel hiked up so high I could see almost everything. "I can't stay in the guest room anymore. It's not right."

I was no longer hearing what she was saying. All my concentration was taken up by her thighs. I grabbed her from around the waist and turned her so she was facing me.

"Please, Sean." She tried to push me away but I wouldn't let her go. I lifted her up and set her on the counter. She grabbed me by the face and pulled me to her lips. I took her towel off. Then, I got out of my clothes.

When it was over, Jessica picked the damp towel up off the floor, covered herself and, without saying a word to me, went into the guest room.

I took a shower then dressed for work. When I sat on my bed to put my shoes on, I saw the laptop on my nightstand. I opened it. Antonio was still there, frozen on my screen.

Shortly after I hired him, he asked me to write a letter to the Department of Immigration and Naturalization Services.

"I'm trying to get my wife out of the Philippines." He sat in a chair in front of my desk, tears in his eyes. "I haven't seen her in five years." He needed me to verify both his income and his good character.

"Type up a letter," I said. "I'll sign whatever you want me to sign." I put a hand on his shoulder. "Don't worry. We'll do everything we can to get her over here."

I pushed play and he came back to life on my screen. He walked to the produce section and stood in front of a barrel of apples. He took one from the bottom, causing a small avalanche. When he bent down to pick them up, his gun fell out of his pocket and hit the floor.

There was a stock boy close by, unloading a cart of watermelons. He was wearing earphones. The reporter from the *Sentinel* suggested that had the stock boy not been listening to music, he might've heard Antonio's gun hitting the floor. And, just maybe, Josephine would still be alive.

I shut the laptop and left for work.

Normally, I'm the first to arrive at the office. But, that morning, when I pulled into the parking lot, almost everyone was already there.

Our secretary, Nancy, pulled into the spot next to mine. She got out of her car and knocked on my window.

"You look like shit," she said when I rolled the window down.

"I had trouble sleeping last night."

"Come on, I'll make you some coffee." She reached in and unlocked my door. From the parking lot, I could see into the office. No one was working. They were all huddled around the common computer. From the looks on their faces, I could tell what they were watching.

"You coming in?" Nancy asked. When I didn't answer, she walked around and got into the passenger's seat. "Have you watched it yet?"

"Not the end."

"I can't believe the *Sentinel* would put that on their website. Just think about that poor girl's family. How they must feel."

"I never would've thought he had it in him."

"His own wife." She shook her head.

"Jessica is leaving me." I turned the heater on.

"Do you want to talk about it?" She adjusted her vent so the hot air was blowing in her face.

"Not really." I started the engine back up. "If Connors calls, will you cover for me?"

"Of course." She leaned over and gave me a small hug. Then, she got out of the car. She was halfway to the front door when she turned around and came back. I rolled the window down. She stuck her head in the car.

"Don't watch the end," she said. "There's no reason for you to see it."

When I came home, Jessica's car was in the driveway. I pulled in behind her and cut the engine. In her backseat, I saw her suitcase and the laundry basket full of clean clothes. In the front, there was a man talking on his cell phone. He was dressed in hospital scrubs. Around his wrist, he had an over-sized gold watch, which caught the sun and sent a ray of light into my eyes.

I stood over the windshield, trying to get his attention. But he pretended like I wasn't there.

The door to the house was wide open. When I walked in, I shut it, then turned the lock.

"Jessica?" I called but got no answer. "Are you home? Jessica?" I went from room to room. "If you're in here, let me know." I could feel the sweat building on the back of my neck. I took my dress shirt off and used it as a towel, blotting the moisture away.

In the bathroom, I splashed cold water on my face. I shoved a handful of nicotine gum into my mouth. So much that, when I tried to call Jessica's name, I couldn't get the words out.

The newspaper was still on the bathmat. It was wet and stepped over but Antonio was still there, his arm around Josephine. I crumbled it into a ball and shoved it into the wastebasket.

I went to the front window. The man in the scrubs was now standing in the driveway. I kept a fire poker by the front door. It was antique, made of rough iron. I picked it up and held it over my shoulder, like a baseball bat. I liked the weight of it, the way it felt in my hands.

I heard a noise coming from the guest room. I left the poker by the front door.

Jessica was lying on the air mattress. She was wearing one of my t-shirts. She had my computer next to her. I could see she had been crying.

"Have you watched this?" She turned the computer so I could see the screen. It was Antonio, in the grocery store.

"I don't want to see any more of it." I took a seat on the mattress and shut the computer. With the back of my hand, I wiped a tear out of her eye.

She took me by the wrist and pulled me down till I was lying next to her. She wrapped her leg around mine. The doorbell started to ring. Then, we heard knocking.

"Shouldn't you get that?" I asked.

"He can wait."

"Who is he?"

"Do you really want to know?" She took my hand and brought it to her lips, kissing my fingers. "You've always had such small hands."

"It's my fingers. I have short fingers."

The longer we ignored the knocking, the louder it got.

The air valve was on Jessica's side of the mattress. She leaned over and released it. We started sinking.

"What if I had asked you to marry me?" I said. "When things were still good."

She pressed her finger to my lips and told me not to talk. We lay there until all the air left the mattress and, underneath us, we could feel the hardwood floor.

I never made it to the end of the video. But I read all about it. Antonio waited in Josephine's line. In front of him, there was an old woman with a cart full of groceries. Also, she had a stack of coupons. It took Josephine a long time to ring her up. She was so consumed in her work, she didn't see Antonio until after the woman settled her bill and pushed her cart away. He didn't offer her a greeting. He just took the pistol out of his pocket.

The police caught up with him in the parking lot. His sweatshirt was stained in blood. They drew their guns and ordered him to put his hands on his head and get down on his knees. He still had the pistol in his hand. He pressed it to his temple and squeezed the trigger.

# Dean Amuck

## *Gary A. Berg*

The University is built on the grounds of a former German engineering manufacturing company from the 1930s. Its brick buildings and dark hardwood paneling make it a natural fit for a college. There are numerous stories about the facility, with website posts claiming a link to Nazi spies laying the groundwork for an invasion of Southern California and secret Germanic sex cults. Even now the campus has an eerie feel, with the too perfect landscaping and orderly appearance. There has always been an undercurrent of tension between the rag-tag 18-22 year old students and the lingering unyielding German order.

The core of the campus consists primarily of the older, brick buildings featuring Escher-like twisting stairways and hallways. I have a large paneled office with a hidden private washroom that opens with an open-palm push. Those that know about the hidden room have left the university and so it has become secret over time. I find myself hiding inside the washroom some afternoons. I sit in the dark of the washroom and listen as people come knocking on my door looking for me.

"I just saw him here a few minutes ago."

"Where did he go?"

Some afternoons I wander over into the long-vacant areas of the inner structure of the campus, those deemed not up to code for students because of handicap access and building material issues. I walk on the old, yet still plush, dark green carpet and hear only softened footfalls. I push a door open and listen to the heavy silence, imagining the previous occupants. What did they see here in the room? What haunted them? Some afternoons I feel a sexual stirring, an unexpected naughtiness. I meet imaginary lovers, co-workers overcome by my desirability, who just have to take off their clothes on the spot. "Oh, Deanie-weenie," they call out passionately, pulling me to the carpet by the pant leg. Their faces are darkened and out of focus, like a video clip hiding the identity of a crime victim.

One thing you can always count on at a university is immobility. If you want to stop something from happening, just sit back. Nothing. It took me a few years to figure out this one simple truth: People around you are happiest if you do nothing. "Just sit there and do nothing," a wise old colleague once told me. And then I learned a slight refinement of the theory, "Act like you are interested, and then do nothing." The "act interested" part was a nice wrinkle. Be "pro-active" (I detest that phrase), and then nothing.

We spend our lives sketching and then erasing the details of ourselves. I discovered this truth in a Bugs Bunny cartoon. I awake each morning and slip on my professional disguise, my university uniform. Khaki pants, button-down shirt and gold tie with university tie clasp, loafers, and blue blazer. The essence of my disguise is the blue blazer. When I work the brass buttons and pull the front close to my belly, I feel my whole body and mind taking on the refrain, the song of myself as a college dean.

One day in a particularly absurd meeting I started to write things down — and I don't ever take notes. Sometimes I secretly record conversations with a tiny digital recorder and then have the library transcribe them as if it is qualitative research. I interview students directly and ask a series of "scientific" questions, which are in fact my own random musings on the spot. The transcription is paid for by a federal earmark. Here forthwith are my research findings now available to you, the reader, for peer review.

INTERVIEW #2014-01

    INTERVIEWER: What is your age?
    SUBJECT: My age?
    INTERVIEWER: Yes, age?
    SUBJECT: I'm a first year.
    INTERVIEWER: Eighteen, nineteen?
    SUBJECT: Twenty actually. I took some time off.
    INTERVIEWER: Do you know what you want to do after college?
    SUBJECT: After college?

And so my interviews go. Until one day, I interview Ramon.

I've seen Ramon around campus. He looks like a middle-aged homeless man. Campus security has stopped him on a number of occasions to question him. But now Ramon is well-known by all on campus and left to be as he is in the great university tradition of extreme tolerance. I suspect he lives in the woods bordering the campus. I've had reports that vagrants have created hideaways, carefully disguising lodgings, rolling sleeping bags and two-man tents away neatly.

With stained hands, Ramon holds out a wrinkled flyer offering a complementary university gift for being an interview subject.

INTERVIEW #2014-02

    SUBJECT: I can use a mug.
    INTERVIEWER: I've seen you riding your bike with the carrier.
    SUBJECT: There is no shoulder on the road. You going to do something about that?
    INTERVIEWER: I've heard that before. Do you live off campus?
    SUBJECT: No.
    INTERVIEWER: Do you eat at the cafeteria?
    SUBJECT: I drink coffee at Denny's and do homework. Last night I had a #1, dry toast.

INTERVIEWER: Do you have financial aid?

SUBJECT: Do you know the Russian matryoshkas dolls? They go one inside the other?

INTERVIEWER: Unhappy with the financial aid process?

SUBJECT: Am I supposed to be happy?

INTERVIEWER: I see.

SUBJECT: I'm happy climbing trees.

INTERVIEWER: Dangerous.

SUBJECT: I found a book on the "Current" shelf in the library called *Extreme Redwood Tree Climbers*. Redwoods don't have branches down low, so they need to either free climb or swing over from another tree. At the top of the tree, there are special plants and insects adapted to living up away from sight.

INTERVIEWER: Must be nice.

I always wanted to be an artist, a painter. But no matter how many studio courses I took, my drawings always had awkwardness to them — "crude" one teacher summed it up. Instead, my career was diverted into academia, art criticism. My dissertation was on the "Kitchen Art Movement" involving found images, a.k.a. dirty sinks. "The Beauty in Everydayness" was the title followed with a heavy colon: "A Structural Analysis of the Kitchen Art Movement, 1960-63."

I still remembered the bitter oral defense in which I was attacked vehemently for excluding portraits of chickens from my study. "How can you omit the most notable folk art movement coming out of American kitchens in the last century?" Dr. Dreyfus spat at me. Of course Dreyfus was an expert on the formal representation of birds in art. Finally, the chair of the committee negotiated a compromise, and I added a half dozen citations referencing Dr. Dreyfus's seminal work.

I spent the early period of my career with spin-off articles on my dissertation and then basically shut down once I had tenure and no further reason to continue the charade of false interest in the topic. I had learned how to act interested while inside my head a chorus of ironic thoughts coalesced. Of course, I did not say what I thought — just occasionally smirked at inappropriate moments in conversations.

INTERVIEW #2014-03

INTERVIEWER: Do you have any idea what you want to do?

SUBJECT: I want to be a social worker.

INTERVIEWER: Why a social worker?

SUBJECT: Because I like helping people out, especially little kids. Because I see some families, and they treat the little kids very badly. Kids belong with a happy family. They should be happy.

INTERVIEWER: Do you know social workers?

I remember hearing Gore Vidal speak in person and an earnest woman stood up and asked him what he recommended to combat writer's block. "Don't write," he said. "The world doesn't need you to write. So if you can't — please don't."

I hate the cliché of failed artists trashing other artists, but can't help myself. The temptation is too great. Sometimes I feel like a bully pulling wings. As with Judith — Judith has talent. A young painter from Vermont who has an easy, unassuming manner. She looks even younger than she is — like a girl. No makeup, usually wears button-down blue men's dress shirts and khaki pants. Her brown hair is stringy; eyes like French roast coffee. Smart too.

At the U. everyone receives tenure sooner or later. Yet the whole process is the basis of much drama. It is the central spectacle of the whole place. It isn't a question of if, but when and with how much fury. Did the Committee give sufficient praise? Did the Dean support? The Provost? The President? What phrase was used in the official letter? "Sufficient," "enough," "minimum," would cause blubbering behind closed doors. "Exemplary," "leader in the field" are posted on office walls.

When Judith's file came to me, I reacted with anger. How dare she ask for promotion so soon! I am old school and believe one has to earn tenure. It isn't a consolation prize. Pay your dues and work your way up. I will speak to her and give her wisdom, my years of experience. But I am frozen, immobile. Finally forced by the Committee to respond, I ask her to coffee.

We meet at the Jungian Mandala coffee shop on campus, decorated with symbols on the walls — a remnant from the 1970s. She comes in and sits down across from me and I am struck by her beauty and effortlessness. She thinks I am giving her good news.

"This is so exciting," she said.

"I don't usually do this."

"I know, and I really appreciate it."

"You may have misunderstood."

"Oh, so sorry."

"No, I should have let you know the context."

She looks directly into my eyes and I avert. "What do you think of my paintings? I am fascinated by your work. I mean I've only seen the older stuff, but love the roughness. It takes a lot of training to look so, so childlike."

"Clumsy, yes, yes."

"I mean primitive."

"I'm afraid I will pass on your promotion for right now."

"Oh, that. I don't care."

"Don't care?"

"Should I?"

"Not if you don't want to."

"Why are you laughing?" she asks.

I dress with a broad-brimmed hat in disguise and set off to wait for Ramon after class. I sit by one of the clinical-looking campus fountains and watch the pre-adult human pageantry flow by. After the entire class seems to have evacuated the lecture hall, I see Ramon pacing with his head down. Ramon then walks carefully from one lamppost in the plaza to the next.

What is he doing?

His pace is unhurried, but purposeful. He does not look at the students who pass him. After going around in a rectangular pattern four times, he stops and sits on a bench. Ramon pulls out a notepad and makes notes.

What is he doing? I have to find out. I stand and walk behind the bench where Ramon sits — his pad is full of squares, all different sizes of squares. I want to stop and look more closely, but don't want to be discovered.

After squaring off the plaza, physically and in his sketchpad, Ramon heads for the edge of campus, which abuts a national forest. As the student crowd thins, I worry that Ramon might notice me. But Ramon walks with his head down in thought and then slips into darkness between two bushy pine trees. I halt at the end of the forest and look back toward the campus. I then push away the branches and walk into the forest.

I pause and let my eyes adjust to the filtered darkness and listen. I hear Ramon's footfall in the distance, straight ahead. The needles and leaves from the tall trees form a thick carpet that deadens footsteps. I move forward quickly, not to lose Ramon. I stop at a tree trunk, bend down and feel the corrugated bark of a redwood tree, and with my other hand I steady myself on the carpet of leaves.

Ramon has stopped ahead at a large pine tree, and begins to climb. I can only see glimpses of him as he quickly makes his way up the tree and then disappears. I stand now safe from exposure peering up. I rub sticky little leaves between my fingers, which gives me an odd sensation. I look down and can make out the burnt red color of poison oak.

INTERVIEW #2014-01B

    INTERVIEWER: Yes, do you have an occupation in mind?

    SUBJECT: I'd like maybe to be a comedian. My friends say I'm funny.

I pull Ramon's class schedule up on the computer screen and pick a time when I know he will be occupied. At the edge of the clearing before the forest, I check behind me and then step into the darkness, now more familiar with my way.

I have prepared in advance this time by bringing something to mark the way — yellow post-it notes. I place the bright yellow paper slips at the base of trees as I walk forward. They immediately prove useful, as I find that I made a wrong turn at some point and have to backtrack. I come across a familiar stone formation and know I am on the right track. Finally I spot the patch of poison oak under a large redwood tree, where I had stood before and watched Ramon.

At the base of Ramon's pine tree, I look around closely to make sure that there is nothing set up to detect or dissuade intruders. I then pull myself up on the first branch which is chest high. As a child I always loved tree climbing but haven't done much of it for years. I enjoy the challenge, the puzzle of placement for feet and hands, and the tactile sensation of gripping the tree and freeing myself from the earth. Once I am about two body lengths up into the tree, the branches become very thick and regularly placed, spiraling upward.

Ramon has discovered a perfect tree for climbing — a natural stairway skyward. All I have to do is step up while at the same time holding onto the branches just above my head. As I make my ascent, I can see that he has cut a few branches out of the way to help form the staircase. Even if he missteps the brush is so thick that the fall would be cushioned almost all the way to the ground. He has picked one of the tallest and thickest trees in the forest.

About two-thirds of the way up, I come to an opening in the branches and find a makeshift home. Ramon has installed flattened cardboard boxes to create a platform. The boxes are for produce and have been wax treated to help with water resistance. Ramon has carefully considered his design. The cardboard is woven expertly and forms a parquet floor effect — it is artistic, almost sculptural. Around the side of the massive trunk, I find a sleeping bag covered securely in a green plastic bag, storage boxes with food items, toiletries, odds and ends. I stop and don't want to look further.

I sit with my back to the trunk, which is remarkably comfortable. I notice above me a piece of canvas is rolled up, perhaps used as a roof on the space when needed. I imagine seeing what Ramon looks at every day. The branches open up on a grand vista of the university's soccer fields. From this position, Ramon can see much of the forest and the playing fields without being seen himself. Something then catches my eye, a reflection in one of the tree tops. I instinctively pull back so that I can't be seen because the light is not something from nature. I peer out again and see the glimmering, like the sunlight off of a mirror or a camera lens. I watch the spot for a while and note that it sparkles as the branches move in the wind — it must be something caught in the tree, not a person. A metallic balloon? Debris from an airplane? Then I notice another sharp light from a tree on the left. It too has the same wind-driven rhythmic flashing. A marker from the forestry service? I wonder what Ramon thinks about when he sees these lights?

I make my way down the tree carefully, trying not to leave any telltale signs of my presence. When I slip into the clearing, I brush off and need to go home to change my sap-stained clothes.

INTERVIEW #2014-04

> INTERVIEWER: What do you want to be when you grow up?
>
> SUBJECT: I'm a Sociology major. What do you mean?
>
> INTERVIEWER: Nobody wants to be a sociologist, really. What do you want to do?
>
> SUBJECT: I want to help people. But I also need to make money. I thought about going into the Peace Corps. Do you know about that?
>
> INTERVIEWER: What makes you think anyone wants your help? What do you bring to the table?
>
> SUBJECT: I like to think I can make a difference.
>
> INTERVIEWER: Have we done you a favor by offering this Sociology major to you?

I need to go to the forest at night. It is the only way to observe Ramon in his natural habitat, like an uncommon bird. I start out just before dusk dressed in black jeans and a long-sleeved tee shirt. All I am missing is a ski mask to complete the look. My one fashion struggle is the shoes — I don't have casual black shoes. I ponder this one in my bedroom before I leave. Do I wear black dress shoes, laced or loafers? Or do I go for the casual brown pair of deck shoes? The deck shoes clearly don't match, but at least they won't slip as much. Also, do I really want to clean caked mud off a pair of dress shoes?

It is a warm, moonlit night. I carry a canvas saddlebag over one shoulder with a sweatshirt and a camera. I think the telephoto lens will come in handy in lieu of a pair of binoculars. Also, I might want to record something for my "study." I look around the clearing on the edge of the forest and wait until random students have their backs to me walking away, and then bend my head and body into the forest cover.

I pause, bend down on one knee, and listen. Nothing. Then attending more closely, an intricate weave of sounds — wind in the trees, squirrels moving in the brush, birds landing and taking off from perches. Then even deeper, the sound of water moving up the trunks of trees, into the branches, the slow decay of leaves and other waste into the thick floor of the forest.

I turn on a small flashlight from my bag and move carefully from one yellow post-it to another. I am careful to step softly in my deck shoes, not wanting to alarm Ramon. When I am about halfway to Ramon's tree, I diverge left, taking the path less traveled, leaving a second trail of post-it notes, this time pink. As I circle round, I keep my eyes on where I think Ramon's tree should be. Sure enough, there is a burnt sienna light in the tree tops, hanging like a Chinese lantern. I stop and look for the best angle through the branches. The telephoto lens works well and pulls the floor of Ramon's makeshift home into focus. I'm too far under the tree to see Ramon and will have to move to the distance.

I walk for another ten minutes in a curved pattern away and then spot a tree similar in density to Ramon's. I spin the shoulder bag around on my back and ascend, hand over hand until I can swing my leg up for a solid foothold. Up I go in the darkness guided by the moon shining like a spoon above me. Two-thirds of the way up, I'm positioned safely across two broad branches. I carefully take out the camera and slip the strap around my neck. I line the camera lens up to where I think Ramon is and find the light, and then his profile. I duck when I find him looking straight back at me in the lens.

How did he spot me? I look around and with the branches above me I'm in complete darkness. He can't see me. Then what is he looking at? I sit up and scan the area in front and then see what Ramon is looking at. About 50 feet in front of me is strung a line of white nylon cord from one tree that I follow across the way. How did that get there?

Suddenly I hear something coming from Ramon's direction, like a bird call. "So-ho! So-ho! So-ho!" Ramon appears to be standing on his platform calling down below. He then stops. I stand up and steady myself by holding onto branches. I spot the white nylon line running from two trees. With my telephoto lens I can see that at the second tree, another line is tied and running off in another direction. I take photos.

Full of myself and my discovery, I climb hurriedly down the tree and follow the nylon cord to the second tree. I then climb that tree up to the line and find where Ramon has tied the cord in a careful knot. I peer out and see that a new line goes on to yet another tree. I take photos. He's made another square. I lean back on the tree trunk in the darkness and catch my breath. I can't see Ramon, but I know he is out there. "Ramon Eno" is the name.

INTERVIEW #2014-06

    INTERVIEWER: Do you feel pressure yourself to do well in school?

    SUBJECT: My parents don't put as much pressure on as I do myself. I put so much pressure on. I always do my best.

I Google Ramon Eno and find he has many pages of links, with large outdoor installations involving ropes, ribbons, lines, and mirrors. He is especially well known in France for audacious conceptual projects which, from the press clippings, seem to provoke extreme reactions, positive and negative.

INTERVIEW #2014-06B

> INTERVIEWER: Is it overwhelming?
>
> SUBJECT: If I don't give everything, why do I waste my time? So it's something, I would like things perfect. And if I don't have it, I try again. If I don't try, I give it up. I like to read motivational books, non-fiction, about how you are motivated to keep going.

I take a leap of faith, into the black forest, diving forward without concern. I pause in the pool of darkness and wait for my eyes to adjust. An owl cries out. Can't see it. Then I'm walking and feel confident that I know the way. I've become a naturalized citizen of the forest.

My foot catches. I trip and fall, and look to my leg — just a vine. I hear footfalls approaching and I'm up and running. At the base of Ramon's tree, I grab hold of the first branches and start up the pine stairway. I'm stopped again and I wrestle out of the grip of a vine and leave a shoe behind.

As I move further and further up the tree, making a great deal of noise as I go, I can see Ramon scurrying around at the top. I stop and listen. "Ramon?"

Silence.

"Ramon, nothing to worry about." I fall back on my normal identity. "I'm with the University."

Silence.

I now slowly make my way up the last twenty feet. I wonder if he has a weapon — not a gun, but maybe a knife? "Ramon? Please don't be afraid. I won't report you."

"What do you want?" Ramon says from behind the massive trunk of the tree above me.

How do I answer? "Can I talk to you?"

Ramon is mute and then moves from behind the trunk and sits on his platform high up in the trees. I ascend slowly up to his tree house. Gasping for breath at the top, I see that he now recognizes me. He gestures to sit across from him, and reaches into a weathered Styrofoam cooler. "Water," he says holding a bottle out to me.

The water tastes like nothing before — fresh, baptismal. We share the stillness.

"Why did you stop making art?" I ask.

"I just wanted to disappear."

"I understand," I say.

"I think you might."

I stand and look out from his platform and see the rope pattern he's created — a web. "You didn't really stop."

Bugs Bunny is one of my favorite people — I consider him a role model. The cartoon that gets me every time is the surreal one entitled Duck Amuck. It's really a Daffy Duck cartoon with Bugs making a cameo appearance at the end. This has to be the deepest, most philosophical cartoon ever made. Daffy is increasingly frustrated as the off-screen animator changes background scenery, and his costumes. He finally confronts the audience: "Hey, who's in charge here?" Daffy's erased with the pink end of a yellow pencil and then redrawn. And then the black scenery pushes in on Daffy, forcing him to prop up the black edges like a heavy curtain. "Who's responsible for this? I demand you show yourself," Daffy yells at the camera at the end. Pull back to reveal over-shoulder Bugs drawing a door to close on Daffy. Bugs turns to the camera, "Ain't I a stinker?" Sketching and erasing. Sketching and erasing.

INTERVIEW #2014-06C

INTERVIEWER: What are your goals?

SUBJECT: I want to go to Harvard Law School and be a public defender.

INTERVIEWER: Harvard is very culturally different. Do you expect adjustment problems?

SUBJECT: Yes, everything is hard. We have to get used to it and adjust. It doesn't matter if you fit, it's something I really want and I've been working so hard for it. So if I get into Harvard I'm going to just do what I'm supposed to do and live with it.

My new bicycle is heavily loaded with blank canvases and paints. Ramon stands near me making the final adjustments to his bicycle and carrier rig. I'm going to have to get in much better shape. We make our way out of the forest down the entrance road away from the university. I'm pedaling slowly, but the wind feels strong under my arms.

# Caryatid

## *Kirie C. Pedersen*

*Goddess guide and protect me.* That is what Diana prayed, in her own manner of prayer. "Diana doesn't believe," Roan accused her at the campus dining hall. That was before Roan moved out of their dorm room to live off-campus with Jack. Before each meal, in that most public of places, Roan insisted they hold hands, close their eyes, and pray. Out loud. If Diana, always ravenous, started to eat, Roan seized her hand across the table. If Diana ignored her or pulled away, Roan prayed anyway.

Witnessing, Roan called it.

Diana believed in privacy, that was all. In the dense Olympic forests or on the black basalt of the Dabob cliffs, the cliffs of her childhood and now, too, her young adulthood, she murmured to the eagles, the great blue heron, the brown warbler, and to the *pinnipeds* just off shore. To the fir and hemlock and cedar with their clusters of bushtits, golden and ruby crowned kinglets, creepers, and nuthatches.

"That's false witness," Roan said. "Nature isn't God."

Yet, when forced to select roommates from the crowd of teenaged strangers, Roan insisted Diana room with her. The four brick towers of the new dorms clustered around an inner courtyard. For meals, they trekked half a mile to a dining hall on main campus, and then back along the same narrow path. Just before the wooded hill in which the new dorms nestled, a tunnel passed beneath the road that led to the art department on main campus. One evening as Diana walked back from dinner alone, dense in her thoughts, she passed into the tunnel and became aware of someone standing at the far end. Her belly went cold.

"*Quien es?*" As always when she walked alone, on campus or in the forests, she thought in Spanish, her refuge from the suffocating barrage of words in classes, in the dorms. She was fairly sure that when she died, her final thoughts would be in Spanish.

And there, squat and solid and beautiful in an oversized flannel shirt, in the almost-dark tunnel with its acrid dripping, thick algae crusting the bricks, was Roan. Someone Diana had barely noticed in the early rush of dorm get-togethers and upper campus treks to meals.

"Room with me," Roan said. Her arms hung heavily at her sides, and her plaid shirt and loose corduroy jeans, men's clothing, seemed to shield her from the autumn coolness. The waning light reflected on her glasses, and Diana could not see her eyes.

Without thinking, Diana shrugged and then agreed. Why not? She had to room with someone.

On her own for the first time in her life, each day seemed more beautiful than the last. On her final day at home, she watched the migratory loons, grebes and mergansers in the middle of the bay, and there, closer to shore, the harbor seals, the *Phoca vitulina,* pups riding on mothers' backs until the mothers rolled them off. The perfect stillness of the salt water, dusk light glimmering on the fall leaves, and then the succulent emerald of salal and *vaccinium ovatum.* The fragrance of salt.

That was spectacular. That was holy.

As she wandered in the forest that final day at home, the trail took a downward turn, and Diana balanced precariously, then tumbled. As her father taught her, she relaxed into the fall.

"That's what we learned in boot camp," he always said, and then her mother scolded him.

"Daddy, she's just a child." Diana liked earning his approval though, dreaming up feats of bravery to draw his always-waning attention. She landed with arms and legs flung out onto the moss, then lifted herself and for a moment stood still, as if testing the solidity of the ground. On the cliffs below, the rocks were sheared by movement along the plates millions of years ago. The drop from cliff to shoreline was no more than fifteen or twenty feet, and sometimes she left the trail here to pick her way down the dark basalt, her feet gripped into crevices. Then she would sit on a dark boulder until the salty water reached her feet.

That day, though, she hoped to follow the trail to its end. In the forest, she never feared the dark. She often hiked by moonlight, trekking across the Olympics, letting her feet sense the path. She was about to turn back when something caught the edge of her vision: a brown shape on a lower abutment of the hackly cliff.

She grasped a slender madrona and leaned as far as she could without falling. Lying on the cobbles at the water's edge was a young deer, spots already fading. Perhaps it was driven from the cliff by hunters shooting illegally or by the dogs that ran in packs at night. In their frenzy to escape, deer would leap straight into space to die, quickly or slowly, as the tide moved in.

Its ears flicked forward, and then back. Diana pulled herself back from the cliff's edge, and this time grasped the branch of a cedar. She stepped into space, and for a moment hung in mid-air. She shifted her weight into the cliff and let the branch fly back upwards. She descended carefully, her hands against the basalt until she stood squarely on the beach six feet from the deer.

She crouched on one knee. "How did you fall?" she asked in a low voice. Its golden-brown body was smooth and flawless. Perhaps it was in shock. She stood and moved a step closer. "You can't just wait for the tide." When she was just a foot away, it leapt to its feet and onto an almost invisible trail. The stones were dark with its shape, with just a slight spotting of red.

With eight children at home, born almost every year with breaks only for miscarriages, Diana's parents took turns in night school, one community college class at a time. Someday, if all went well, they would become teachers. If Diana, their eldest, wanted to attend college, she would have to figure it out on her own. Fill out and sign the forms. Babysit. Waitress. Wash the private parts of dying elders in a retirement home. But even working since she was fifteen and a half, she'd saved only enough for the first quarter's tuition.

The new dorms she'd managed to get into at the last moment clung to the edge of a hillside. When they dropped her off in the muddy parking lot, Diana's parents didn't get out of their battered black and red Volkswagen bus. Holding her satchel of books in one hand, her backpack of clothes in the other, she looked at the dorm towers. They seemed like stacked boxes, raw brick not yet seasoned by weather. Mattresses were stacked, encased in plastic, beside a dry fountain.

Roommates were supposed to be assigned, but many parents had taken one look and driven off again, offspring safely in tow. Growing up in a home where she never had space of her own except in the forests, Diana hoped to remain alone. She unpacked four pots of moss she dug from the forest floor early that morning and placed them on the desk, and then sat on the floor in the dark, savoring her arrival.

When the suicides started, not that far into the quarter, nobody was supposed to know, but of course word traveled quickly. They jumped, Roan said. It was hard to figure out how anyone could die jumping from a fourth floor balcony. Diana didn't have time to think much about it because she desperately needed a job. She applied to serve breakfast at the food service, and soon was rising at four to stand behind a heated cart offering up bacon and pancakes and hot cereal to her classmates. She asked around, and soon, on Fridays and Saturdays, she was babysitting for three of her professors. The professors and their wives always invited her for dinner first, everyone sitting around the table, candles lit, books lining the walls.

The pale cement and brown-red brick of the dormitories glowed in the autumn sunsets. On the fourth floor of the tower catching the day's last light, a tall young man stood alone in the uncarpeted hallway. He tapped at a door on the far end of the hall. When he heard no sound from inside, he pushed at the door, and then he ducked inside.

Michael's first impression was that the room was so fucking tidy. Immaculate. Almost sterile. In the window, she'd hung a ceramic mobile composed of three circles of graduated size, each suspended by string from a piece of bleached driftwood. The small student desk was covered with small boxes lined with some kind of dirt and moss. Above the desk, the bulletin board held photographs of animals: a cat, a fawn, and a white bearded goat. Beside the desk was a bookcase made of boards and bricks. The top shelf held texts for botany, chemistry, ornithology, and biology, while the middle poetry, plays, philosophy, and ancient literature. The bottom held Spanish texts: grammars, novels, and philosophy, held erect by a broken clay Buddha head. He leaned down and picked it up, tossing it from one hand to the other, and the green paint flecked off in his hands.

The mattress was placed on the floor, covered with a bright green quilt and stacked with mustard-colored cushions. A low table held a work schedule from the food service, another from the college print shop, and a hand-written budget with items ranging from cups of tea to rent. At the head of the bed was a cheap Modigliani print tacked directly into the wall.

"Are you taking photographs in case we get lost?" she had asked that first day when Michael shot images of each new student. "In case we disappear and nobody can find us?" And then she ducked her head and vanished into the dorms.

It was his roommate, Adam, who dared him. They should select three of the new girls. See if they could make them commit suicide. Whoever seemed most fragile or vulnerable or innocent.

Late that night, someone tapped at the door. Diana still had trouble figuring out the system in the dorms. There was supposed to be some kind of security, but as with everything else, it didn't seem to work. At home, isolated in the forest, they'd never even locked the doors.

"Who is it?"

"Jack."

Diana sucked in her breath. She had not seen Jack since breaking up with him the first week they arrived. She wanted to concentrate on school, she said. And work. But then, when he and Roan paired up, she was devastated. Maybe she was just homesick for her family, for the forest and the beach and what she knew, or maybe just overwhelmed by school and then work, but she couldn't stop crying. Or wanting to die, that thought arriving unbidden with every in-breath and exhalation. In the tiny cluster of dorms, and even on main campus, Jack and Roan were always visible, huddled together, a community of two.

"The door's not locked," Diana said.

"You need to lock it," Jack said. He paced around the room as if to examine the space Roan inhabited, then vacated, as if to cast judgment on Diana's failure even at this, the keeping of a friend. His shirt was dirty, one elbow torn out, and his fly was caught on his shirt. His hair was dirty too. She started to say something about his shirt, but then caught herself. She gestured towards the single chair by her desk.

"Have a seat," she said. Instead, Jack slid onto the low table by the bed, knocking her budgets and books to the floor.

"How are you?" He spoke in a mock-crooning manner, as if swallowing his own words. His glance skidded across her. If he cared how she was, why hadn't he come to see her before now?

"I'm just fine," she said. "Looking for more work."

He turned quickly, half-sliding off the table. "Let's cut the shit," he said. "I'm here for a reason."

Diana's stomach clenched. So he was in one of those moods. She had heard him turn that icy voice on friends, and then, at the end, to her. He picked up the broken Buddha head she used to prop her books and tossed it from one hand to the other. It had been his first gift to her.

"Roan and I are engaged." Diana nodded as if she already knew, had always expected this. He paused as though it was now Diana's turn to say something, but she continued to nod, a mirror of the head passing from one palm to the other, a nodding fool. "Roan lets me be who I am." Jack went on and on, and she wanted to tell him to cut the shit, but instead she stopped listening. He could talk for hours like this, never looking at the person he was talking to. At her.

"So what are you studying?" she finally asked. As if he was just any student she was meeting on campus.

"I dropped out." Jack set the Buddha head back onto the shelf. "I'm going into the ministry."

"What?" Jack had never expressed the slightest interest in what he deemed conventional religion. "Where?" She was the mistress of monosyllables.

"I'm going to work in the ghetto," he said. *The ghetto.* Where was that coming from? The word, in his mouth, seemed false. "So my dad cut me off, but Roan's willing to work to put me through."

"You're having an actual wedding?"

"We believe in ceremony."

Diana gestured to her tiny room, the Buddha head and the mosses. "I believe in ceremony," she said.

Jack raised his hand as if he wanted to punch her. "To you, people are objects. You collect experiences like some people collect postage stamps."

"Jesus, dude."

The door opened, and there was Michael, that photographer guy who recently helped Diana carry a box of books to her room and then stayed for a cup of tea. Diana had found herself telling him she was raised, isolated, on the commune, and how devastated she was when her boyfriend slept with her roommate. Michael had listened, nodding. He was shy, she thought.

Now he strode into her room as though he owned it.

Jack held out his hand and Michael stood for a moment, allowing Jack's arm to hang in the air. Then he reached out and tapped Jack's palm. Jack settled back onto Diana's bedside table.

"Can I use your phone?" Michael asked. "Mine's dead." Without waiting for her reply, he snatched her phone from the desk and stepped into the tiny bathroom that opened off the entry.

"And that is?" Jack asked.

"My friend," Diana said. And maybe he was. Although she wished both of them would leave.

And they did, Jack shortly after Michael, who emerged from the bathroom, dropped her phone back onto her desk, and hurried out. Diana lit a candle and switched off the light. Jack was right. She wasn't normal. She was happy to be free from the weight of someone else's moods and needs. With Jack, she had wanted to make love slowly, whatever it took with someone her own age, far from the groping fingers of her father's drunken friends. And he had started out that way, touching her gently, but then she became frightened, frozen, and he became angry.

And then, Roan. Roan didn't see him as an object, a postage stamp. Roan was willing to commit her life to him, to work to put him through.

Michael had left her a drawing. It was a nude, hands clasped to belly. Diana didn't like it, but it was kind of a gift, she supposed, and for a while she left it sitting there.

She was taking Spanish 311, Entomology, Ancient Literature, and Field Botany. She was already thinking about majoring in forensic entomology, although she also liked botany and of course, always, Spanish. In one of her classes, they watched a documentary on migrants, and when the instructor asked for volunteers to tutor at the migrant center, she raised her hand. So now she was tutoring Graciela, a long ride in a college van every Tuesday night. And the food service and the print shop and three babysitting gigs for professors. The guy at the print shop, Bill, asked if she was interested in art modeling. Over at the art department. Roan did that and said it was easy money.

Just sit or stand or lie there, or whatever, she said. Boring.

Diana couldn't imagine being naked in front of strangers, but it was already time to pay next quarter's tuition and housing, and the cost even for used books had knocked her out. She worked at least five hours every day, more on weekends, and she studied eight or ten hours or more, sometimes all night. Her eyes felt as if they were falling out of her head, but she couldn't afford glasses. She was exhausted all the time. And she hadn't even had a chance to ride her bike, alone, into the mountains.

Yet every morning when she woke on her narrow mattress, she was smiling. She loved college. I'm in my prime, she told herself. My real life is starting. She wanted to read every book for every class. She wanted to learn all the plants and birds and insects and everything else the sea and forest and, really, the whole wide world had on offer.

"How's the work-study going?" Michael asked. He seemed to be waiting on the stairs, even to know she was one of the rare students who used them, but Diana shrugged off her uneasiness. She was wearing a skirt, unusual for her, and she felt awkward. She had been up since dawn, first to serve breakfast, and then to log in five hours at the printery. Then class.

"I need to earn more money," she said.

"You like the print shop?"

"It's okay. Easier than I thought it would be." Michael had been the one to tell her when the position opened, and for some reason she'd thought the work would be more art-related. She jiggled her fingers in the air. "It's just machines that line up pages and these monster staplers."

"Most jobs sound better than they are."

"That's what Jack said."

"He's a slick-looking dude." She had no desire to discuss Jack with Michael or with anyone, and she didn't want to be around Michael, really, but here she'd let him follow her up to her room.

"Did you like the drawing I left?"

Diana didn't want to say she'd thrown it away, that it gave her the creeps. "What does it mean?"

"It reminds me of you."

"That's a compliment?"

"She doesn't want anyone to touch her. She takes long walks alone. Other women would be frightened."

"Tell me about your classes," Diana said. Get them talking about themselves, her mother had always said, and Diana wanted to deflect Michael's demand for the center of energy. "Mine are hard." Spanish in particular was hard. She hadn't studied Spanish since ninth grade, but she learned best by pushing herself, the same leap Graciela had to make. If she had her way, Spanish would be the only language she would speak. *Suenos* were dreams. *Sonador* a dreamer. The dreaming ones.

Michael was talking. He never knew his father, he said, was brought up by his mother in a black neighborhood. *The ghetto.* That word, again. He wanted to work in the arts. Or politics. As he spoke, his face contorted. He never stopped moving, his hands plucking at his face or hair. His lips were thick, and sometimes they seemed ugly, even repulsive, and for moments, they seemed sensual.

"What does it take to get into politics?" Michael's words had finally run down, and he sat there grimacing. Although Michael wasn't volunteering at the migrant center, he started in about farmworkers.

"You fat cats sit around," he said.

"I'm not a fat cat," Diana said.

"You're white," Michael said.

"So are you."

"I grew up in the ghetto."

"I grew up in squalor," Diana said. "My parents are dirt poor. They'll be thrilled to stop being laborers and teach school. If they ever make it."

"But happy," Michael said. "I'll bet you were happy."

Jack and Michael both seemed so nice when she met them, and then as soon as she allowed them into her life, they became angry, as though she embodied everything wrong in the world, everything that held them back. Or was it just sex, and that she didn't want to be with them?

"I read my bank statement yesterday," Diana said. "I won't make it through the month." She looked down at her cuticles, torn and edged with blood. "I'm tired."

The next morning as she waited for a bus back from main campus, a man pulled over and offered her a ride. When she refused, he became mean, as if he was going to force her into his car. "No thanks, no thanks," she said, politeness her default.

"Get in," he said, menacing now. Diana ducked into a bookstore. Then she froze. Jack and Roan were at the check-out. Their bodies arched as they faced each other in the midst of some intense conversation. Roan's glasses sat lopsided on her nose, and her hair was ragged, uncombed. Diana ducked back onto the street and walked back to the dorms. She was fine. This was what she had wanted: to be alone, a community of one. Yet something felt injured, and the feeling would not go away.

She called her mother to ask for a small loan to tide her over. "If you can," she said. She had never asked her parents for money.

"We put ourselves through," her mother said. "You can do the same."

Without knocking, Michael walked into her room. "I don't want to like you," he said, and then walked back out. A few moments later, he returned. "I want to fuck you," he said. He knocked the boxes of moss to the floor.

The next day at the print shop, she told Bill she needed more hours. "I thought I'd make more here," she said. "I can't even make tuition for next quarter." She told him she could babysit. "I'm working for three professors if you need references."

"I told you I have something better," Bill said. "A buddy and I have a photography gig."

"I don't know anything about photography."

"As a model."

"I don't have any experience." Though Diana thought again of Roan, how easy she said it was.

"We don't want phony," Bill said. "We want real." He mentioned an amount that was more than she'd ever earned in her life, for any kind of work. Bill ran his hand through his hair. "How's Saturday at ten? I'll pick you up."

"Oh, I can walk," she said. The art department was just off the walking path between main campus and her dorm.

"I'll give you a ride." He smiled.

At ten on Saturday morning, Diana waited in the muddy parking lot behind the dorms. At ten-fifteen, she was about to return to her room when a battered green Chrysler pulled up beside her. A man leaned his head out the window. "Bill couldn't make it today. He's real sorry. Hope that's okay." The man did not look like an artist. He had short dark hair, like someone in the military. The car seemed weird too, though she couldn't quite say why. Then she thought about how nice Bill was, and how she didn't want to let him down. Or seem stupid to just turn around, turn her back on the money, like some scared little girl.

The man leaned over and shoved open the passenger door. Inside the car, Diana felt very small. The man talked on and on, almost as if she wasn't there. The business. Being an artist. One of these days he and Bill would make it big, get out of the eight to five shithole. Soon they would meet Bill, or would Bill be there? She realized he hadn't said. The man wore tight jeans and a short-sleeved shirt, and on his forearm was a tattoo, a coiled cougar, like those she used to see, dead, in the back of pick-up trucks when she was growing up.

When the man turned left toward the town instead of right toward the art building, Diana said nothing. It was as if she'd forgotten how to speak. It seemed they drove a long way, turning and then turning again in the town Diana had not yet explored, and Diana quickly lost track of where she was.

Finally the car entered what seemed a rough part of town, broken-down cars and trucks on the street, and plastic children's toys in the yards, the houses with faded and peeling paint. The man slid the car into a space in front of a small house almost directly beneath the expressway. Traffic roared overhead. The dog chained to a small plywood structure lifted its head as the car pulled in, and then thumped it back onto the ground and closed its eyes.

Part of what the man had talked about so ceaselessly during the drive was his wife and kids, and Diana had convinced herself she was safe. But as he opened the front door to the house, he said "The wife and kids are visiting Grandma." The living room was empty except for a sofa, a camera on a tripod, and a television with the sound turned off. "Cup of coffee before we get going?" She nodded. Yes. Coffee. So innocent. Nobody intending to hurt her would offer coffee.

He gestured toward a small kitchen, and Diana sat at a small plastic table. He poured a cup of coffee for her and popped open a beer for himself. "Would you like to see some of our work?" It took a moment for Diana to register what he meant, and then, again, she nodded. He pulled out a photo album with a plastic cover, the kind anyone might have, but when Diana opened it, the pages were empty. "Damn," he said. "I forgot I sent everything to my mom. Well, here's the kind of stuff I want to do." He opened a glossy hardbound book filled with images of beautiful young women, girls really, lying in grass and under trees.

She needed to tell him she wanted to leave. This was all a misunderstanding, a mistake. He wasn't an artist, and she wasn't a model. But she had forgotten how to form words.

The man stood. "Let's cut the shit," he said. "You can get ready here, or would you feel more comfortable in there?"

Comfortable? She looked at the doorway of the room where he had pointed. Yes. She would go in there. It was a small bedroom, like a child's room, only there was no evidence of children. She closed the door behind her and then she sat on the bare mattress for what seemed a long time. The only window was small, high on the wall above the bed, the sill and frame coated with thick slimy dust.

"What's keeping you?" he said at last, and then he opened the door.

Diana was still trembling. It was as if her hands and body belonged to someone else. She sat beside the small window of her dormitory room.

*Make it real, baby.* That was the way he had talked, and still, she never spoke, just counted the flashes of his camera. You're beautiful. Make it real.

When he dropped her off in the parking lot, he was still talking. He took one final shot, he said, a single tear running down her face. And then he reached into his pocket and threw some money at her, a few crumpled bills.

That was what she was worth.

How could she still be alive? Maybe she was actually dead. She moved to her mattress on the floor, leaned back, and then hit her head against the wall. She was alive, then. If her body didn't hurt so damn much, maybe she could think.

She became aware of someone behind her.

"Did you know I paid you a little visit last night?" Michael spoke as though continuing a conversation started some time before. When Diana didn't respond, he spoke more loudly. "Did you hear what I said? I came and paid you a little visit." Diana stared toward the window, though she could see nothing. Michael's voice, like that of the stranger, went on and on but she heard only sounds. Finally she heard herself speak, but in such a quiet voice Michael had to lean over to hear her.

"I was raped," Diana said. She was touched by evil, and the evil must be shining on her face for Michael, for everyone to see.

He smiled. He did not reach out to touch or comfort her. "Everyone gets raped."

"This isn't a metaphor," Diana said.

But Michael was not to be stopped. Still without looking at her, he spoke as if reciting poetry. Some get raped over and over, he told her. Some women are just losers, and they clamber to their feet only to be raped again.

From the new distance she felt between herself and all living things, distance from the world itself, Diana watched him. Dimensions shifted. Altered. Now Michael formed the shadow around the edges of the photograph. "I knew a girl raped by her uncle," he said. "She killed herself." Michael said she was Candy, Lolita. That she wanted to be hurt. That she, Diana, was now evil, and from this day on, everyone would despise her.

Everything in the room, its dimensions, shifted again, and Michael seemed far away. She herself was minute, the size of a tendril of moss on a forest trail.

"You need to leave," she said. And then, for the first time, she locked her door.

That night, sounding drunk, Michael returned. When he tried the door and found it locked, he began to pound. "This is no way to run a whorehouse," he shouted. "You fucked someone. Now you might as well fuck me." She wondered what the other students thought, if someone would emerge from a room to stop him. But after all, in the dorms, shouting and weeping and the sounds of breaking glass were not that unusual. Just another Saturday night.

It was as if she carried weights: weights on her arms, her legs, her skull, her chest. It was hard to keep walking and talking, to go to classes, to babysit small children. She felt soul-scraped and foul. She wrote her composition for Spanish, seven pages. She pressed and labeled spores of the mosses, lichens and liverworts she was studying in lab. She studied for exams. She sat through class, listening as each student presented a project, but everyone seemed to be playing a game. Everything people did or said around her, in class or in the crowded dining hall, seemed inane, pointless, and inexplicable. She desperately wanted to talk with someone, but there was no one to talk to. There was a mist between her and other people. Suffocating now in the tiny room, she rode her blue bicycle to the top of the hill where the college was perched, and then streaked straight down.

An ecstasy ride, she used to call it.

At the bindery, she saw Bill but managed to avoid him through morning. Then, when no one was around, he approached her work station. "How did it go?" he said. He leaned closer and spoke straight into her hair. "I hear you have beautiful breasts," he said. Diana felt as though insects were crawling across her skull, and a quick sharp pain in her belly. She began to sweat from her lips and forehead, and her head felt heavy. She picked up her backpack and ran out the door.

The following morning, she was serving breakfasts when it happened again. There was the usual rush, the line of early morning eaters. She glanced out at her fellow students and again the insects crawled across her scalp, with one quick sharp pain in her belly. She ran back into the kitchen, clutched the wall, and fell. A workman there to repair the stoves, his hands steady, helped her into the office. Her legs were shaking too much to walk. Other students looked at her as if embarrassed for her.

She wanted to be held by her mother. She felt like a small helpless child, her voice high and trembling.

"I'm okay," she said. "I'll go to my room."

Diana lay on the narrow mattress. Then she heard a huge roar outside, and she went to the window. A dump truck poured great mounds of topsoil into a break in the pavement. Perhaps someone would plant a tree there, or a shrub, or wildflowers.

She wanted to dig her hands into that earth and crouch huddled at the bottom.

Diana felt she'd half-died, but only just half; she remained alive. A man could not understand what it was like unless he'd been raped himself, to be entered like that and pounded and bruised so deeply inside your body. The physical pain was deeper than previous injuries, a broken wrist or pneumonia or migraine. She now lived in two worlds, real and unreal, dream and reality. The forest, where she grew up, was called unreal. "You must get out into the world," her high school teachers had told her when they urged her to apply for college. But the forest, the shore was more real because she could eat food she collected herself, sleep when it was dark and wake at dawn. The books she'd read so eagerly for classes now meant something different. What did Novalis say? When we dream that we dream we are beginning to wake up. She dreamed she dreamed the rape, but it happened. And here she was, still serving ninety-four breakfasts every morning and reading about Juan Manso or the *Hombre Ideal* in Spanish, buying a pen or writing a paper. Eating in the food service. It was a shock, how the body kept going. Already the bruised tissue was beginning to heal; the scratches disappeared. The tears had dried immediately, but tears were immortal anyway; the earth, Mann said, was made of tears.

And how would her spirit heal? What would this do to her life? She knew she was still in shock; blanked-out, mostly. Greened-out, for as she drifted back to consciousness she watched lichens and mosses on the periphery of her vision. She felt like a shriveled shrunken person. Her father always said she was foolish. She had been foolish to take the job. See what a fool I am Dad.

She died, but she was still alive, and that was what she wanted to say: I am still alive.

If she could conceive of a different world, then that world existed, if only in her mind. She felt as if she was just walking along one day, and then she changed to dust. Or liquid. Her legs had melted, her arms had melted, her face had melted. A young girl was walking along in her life one day, and she melted.

She packed a few things into her backpack, jumped onto her bicycle, and headed off campus and along a rural country road. She found a trail that led deep into the woods, and followed it. Then she gathered stones to form a circle, tinder and broken logs to build a fire, and she cooked a potato in the coals. She ate with her fingers, savoring the steaming heat. In the forest, she heard a shrill howl. A bobcat maybe. Sweat poured down her face, but she had no fear. For the first time in a week, she felt safe.

When she awoke before dawn, the coals were still warm. The rising sun lit the edges of the trees. As if enlivened by first light, the bushtits, kinglets, creepers, and nuthatches darted from branch to branch, each in its own way yet protected by the flock from predators. It was spring, and she would finish her classes, and soon enough, the quarter would end.

In June, Diana returned to her parents' house and resumed her high school jobs, her role in the family. When Michael called to say he wanted to talk, she didn't much care. "I need to make amends," he said.

"Amends," she said, as if tasting the word.

"Not for you," he said. "For myself." He told her about the pact. He and Adam were bored, he said, and they picked out three girls in the incoming class they believed to be most vulnerable. And pretty, he added, as if that might console or comfort her.

"You thought I was vulnerable?" Diana sipped at her tea. Her plans and her life stretched out before her. Even though work with the old people was hard, devastating sometimes, and the drunks at the cafe be crude and abusive, she was glad to wake up each day. "Who were the others?" When he named them, Diana laughed. "We three are the strongest," she said. What she wouldn't say was that he wasn't worth that much to her, that she refused to allow him or anyone to force her from life. That she remained alive for lichen like a cameo, a minute imprint hidden within softness. For rain that seemed to fall from a single edge just beyond sight. For the green tinge on one side of a madrona, struck golden as the sun set behind the hill.

To live on. That was it. Not something, Diana saw, that he could

75

understand. Nor was it her job to fix or forgive, him or anyone. Roan and Jack seemed equally small, just as she herself had seemed small when she wanted to die. The rapist still seemed huge and terrifying, but still, she now felt a looseness, as if she had jumped out from a ditch and was stumbling along. Camus said you needed great falls to learn what you didn't want. That horror she'd never wanted for herself or anyone else, but still, she was alive for her own form of rapture.

In botany, she'd learned that a biome or natural community completed steps and changes, ending in its climax. This was called a sere. Her own sere had been her childhood in the forest, where, for a brief moment, she prospered. But seedlings cannot grow in immense shade, and so the lofty trees died, and the delicate balance changed. But never did it begin again from scratch, for the dying trees fed the soil. New life grew on the leaf mold of the old. The common definition of sere *was dried up, withered.* These, she saw now, were simultaneous definitions, the climax of a forest life, and the kind of death from which new life begins.

# Too Big to Carry

*Tara Isabel Zambrano*

I am a car salesman and not a man of big words. The car dealership where I work is about a fifteen minute driving distance from my home. There are many small businesses in between. Donut shops, a deserted factory, gas stations, and hair and tattoo salons. A town named *Detroit*, another *Miami*. All in Texas country. There is one called Lovelady. Whenever I pass through that town, it makes me wonder if I were a poet, perhaps I could write something magical about it.

I am a Baptist. I grew up not too far from where I live now. On my way to work, I see signs like, "Jesus is Lord," or, "Jesus died for your sins," and it strengthens my belief that I'm in the right place, and I am dealing with my own kind. It is good for business and good for me.

My wife comes from a Baptist family too. She is devoted to me and to Sean, our only child. It took a long time for her to conceive. Drugs, IVs and painful procedures. When my son was born, he was diagnosed with a rare spinal disorder. He cannot walk or move; he stays in bed all day and my wife stays by his side, talking to him as if someday he is going to get up and go on with his life like he missed nothing.

I must confess that I don't talk much to her and there have been occasions when I don't talk at all. At night when she comes closer to me, I feel her heart pressed against my arm — fast and furious. She falls asleep with her mouth open and her face flat in the darkness. I can still feel the light tremors of the day. As if she has pushed her feelings to the far end of her body, and now they are slowly resurfacing. I don't move for hours so as not to disturb her, but if there is an itch or a sneeze, I just wince, reminding myself that there is a nose on my face, feet at the end of my legs.

Sometimes after a long day, when I reach home, she is standing at the front gate. She grabs the keys of our car and takes off without saying a word. I walk inside and play with my boy, feed him and change him. He always smiles when he looks at me. Then I lie in bed waiting for her, and she comes home and lies down next to me. I hold her in my arms, my foot rests over hers, and she buries her head in my shoulders, her warm tears seeping into my T-shirt, touching my skin. She says that our son has grown too big for her to carry. She needs help. I don't console her, because I know that she will shake off my consolation as if a mosquito has just buzzed her ear. And I don't make any promises to her, because I'd be lying. Only a man who knows how to fill hope and beauty in mundane things such as how a bird takes flight, or a spider weaves his web, or how a mother tends to her only child, can do that. So I take her in my arms and we make love with the ease that I always felt with her, right from the

77

start. While I am still inside her, hard and moving, she comes, shivering, then growing limp and loose, waiting for me to come so that she can stop moaning. I move over and she turns, facing me, and falls asleep. And her expressionless face makes me wonder if I know this woman I love so much. If someday, I may betray her by not understanding her. I run my fingers through her hair, realizing that she hasn't had a haircut in a long time. It has been a while since she applied makeup and painted nails like she used to before we got married. My thoughts wander into the orbit of my job, and I think about getting a car for her, probably a Toyota, considering her petite frame, but I don't think she will ever accept that. Not a Japanese car, for sure.

There are days when I come home early after making a sale. I cook and she takes a bubble bath. Then we sit outside with our son in our lap and watch the trees and the birds. Sitting side by side with her, I feel like my wife and I are like two rivers — crossing and separating, with fertile deltas in between. We keep flowing, knowing the other is right beside us, even if we don't get to see each other for most of the day. And in the absolute certainty of those moments, something I can never describe perfectly, I want to run in the backyard with my son in my arms, like a new car, its paint still wet, with its windows down, speeding on the back roads. While my wife laughs and claps, we go faster, my son clinging to me with all his strength, and I feel my chest — first tight with exhaustion but growing lighter. The small space inside me expands and merges into the world outside, and nothing seems too heavy anymore. I float like a balloon filled with what I think is called happiness.

## EDITORS' PRIZE:
# Elmo in the Passenger Seat

### *Michael P. Adams*

I used to live under the sign that said "Piñatas," where I learned pretty quickly that it didn't pay to make friends. The number of my paper-covered brethren that came and went was staggering, but I was always left behind. Don't get me wrong: I'd still talk to the others, especially the older ones that seemed to be in it for the long haul like me. But the new ones — the popular ones who barely lasted a day before they were snatched up and replaced by another — I didn't bother reaching out to them. It just wasn't worth the effort.

I've never heard what happens when one of us gets picked, although I thought I was finally going to find out a few weeks ago when a girl came in with her mother.

"How about this one?" the mother said, pointing at me. If I had insides, they definitely would have been swirling.

"Uh-uh," the kid said.

"Why not?" The woman fondled the tag on my foot and seemed to like what she saw. "I think we should get this one."

"No, mommy. Elmo is for babies."

"I thought you liked Elmo."

"Not anymore. That one's got a weird head anyway. It's all smashed in on one side. I want SpongeBob."

The mother looked at SpongeBob's tag, sighed, and relented. My deformed head and I were left behind once again.

After that, the only person who touched me was the store's manager when he moved me to my new home: the clearance rack. It was lonelier, but not nearly as bad as I'd thought. I was getting noticed a lot more, though I didn't always know who was looking at me. The manager had covered my right eye — my good eye — with a sticker. So it wasn't until I landed on the cashier's counter that I knew someone had finally selected me. What an honor! I couldn't wait to see who it was that thought me worthy of bringing into their home. It was a man. I knew that much from the voice. And he was strong; I could feel the muscles in his arm as he carried me out, squeezing me too tightly. When he propped me up in the passenger seat of his truck, I got my first look at his face.

He looked angry, jaw clenched, eyebrows furrowed, and I took it personally. Maybe I wasn't worthy. Maybe he only picked me because I was cheap or because it didn't take any extra thought to pluck me off the clearance rack. I had made a horrible first impression, and he hated me already.

"Elmo," I heard a child say behind me.

"Quiet, Reagan," my new dad said. I thought it was strange that I hadn't seen or heard this child earlier. Parents always brought their kids into the store with them. This one seemed to have been left in the car alone.

"See Elmo," Reagan said.

"Not right now. I'm driving."

"Elmo, Daddy. Elmooooooooo!" He got louder, more screechy, every time he said my name. If I had never been exposed to a child's expression of excitement, I might have thought that he hated me, too.

"Enough!" Dad reached back; the sound of a smack was followed by the child's wail.

I had sat on the shelf long enough to see my share of spoiled kids and the exasperated parents who felt the need to hit them, but I never imagined that was the type of parent I'd be going home with one day. Since I hadn't actually seen anything, I tried to give Dad the benefit of the doubt. Maybe what I heard wasn't a smack. Maybe Reagan dropped something and Dad reached back too late to catch it. What I heard was a toy hitting the floor, and that's why Reagan was crying. I knew I was kidding myself, no matter how much I wanted it to be true.

"Stop crying, Reagan," Dad ordered. I'm not even sure Reagan could hear him over his sobbing. Dad tried again, louder this time. "I said stop crying." The boom in his voice seemed to signal to Reagan that he wasn't messing around anymore, and Reagan started to calm down.

I felt terrible. It was my fault that Reagan got hit. If he hadn't gotten so wound up when he saw me, Dad wouldn't have raised a hand to him. I had waited my whole life to bring a child joy, and I'd done the complete opposite. Add it to my list of failures: deformed head, reduced price, betrayer of children. If I could, I would have hurled myself out of the car right then and there.

As we pulled into the driveway, I marveled at the house I'd be living in, a definite upgrade from the party supply store. Two stories, lush landscaping, brick chimney, a wreath of flowers on the front door. How could such a bad man live in such a wonderful place?

"Have Elmo, Daddy?" Reagan asked, his voice still shaky, not yet recovered from all the crying.

A moment later, Dad's big hand was palming my head as he took me out of the car and passed me off to Reagan. Without saying a word, Dad went inside the house. He left the front door open for Reagan, and we slowly made our way toward it, a bumpy ride for me. Reagan and I were the same height, which meant that our walk to the house was full of unintentional kicks in the shins and a near-drop when Reagan got to the front step. But we made it inside, my new hero and I, and he stood me up on the kitchen floor. Reagan studied my face, his little mouth hanging open, his fingers caressing my dented head. He started to pick at the sticker over my eye, his gentle scrapes the most care anyone had ever taken with me. My sight was restored in stages as Reagan tore the sticker off piece by piece. Then, SLAM!

"Reagan! Why didn't you close the front door?" I could feel Dad's voice reverberating through the floor. "Where are you?"

Reagan scurried away, ducking inside a cabinet where he pushed through pots and pans to make himself fit. He was seconds away from safety when Dad came in, grabbed his arm and yanked him out of the cabinet. I wish I had had stickers over both eyes so I didn't have to see the spanking that followed. Six hard whacks to Reagan's behind and a crying jag that I expected to last until the next day. I was crying, too, in spirit.

"How many times do I have to tell you to close the door? And don't try to hide from me. That only makes it worse." Then he did something I wasn't expecting. He crouched down and kissed Reagan's cheek. "I'm sorry that you make me so mad. Remember the rule: two minutes and you're done crying." Dad set the timer on the stovetop. Reagan scooted over next to me and cried into my dent, dropped a tear on my shoulder. I didn't mind at all.

Mom was nice. She got home just as Reagan was about to be put to bed. Running to greet her in his red footie pajamas, Reagan let out what had to be the world's cutest laugh (the first I had heard from him all day). Seeing him so happy, all in red no less, gave me a vicarious thrill; I imagined that's what I would look like if I could run. Mom knelt down, accepted Reagan's embrace.

"I missed you so much today," she told him.

"Story, Mommy?"

"Okay, sweetie. Give Daddy a kiss." She carried him over to Dad, who took his lips away from his Budweiser can just long enough to press them against Reagan's forehead.

"Say nigh-nigh, Daddy," Mom prompted.

"Nigh-nigh," Reagan said. "Nigh-nigh, Elmo."

Mom looked down at me. "This is the piñata?" she asked Dad.

"That's it," he said.

"It's kind of — "

"Nigh-nigh, Elmo," Reagan repeated, as if he were waiting for me to respond. Never have I wanted to speak more than at that moment, to let Reagan know how much it meant that he cared about me.

"You want to bring Elmo to your room?" Mom asked.

"Yeah," Reagan said.

She carried us upstairs, set me down next to Reagan's crib. They got settled in the rocking chair, and Mom read us a story about a runaway bunny whose mother always manages to find him.

Reagan fell asleep quickly, but not before chanting my name about a hundred times. Could this kid be any more adorable? I was glad he was saved from having to hear what I heard going on downstairs.

"You said you'd be home earlier tonight."

"I know. I'm sorry. Dale's got a presentation on Monday that he needed some help with. It was either stay a little later today or go in over the weekend. I texted you."

"Yeah, I got it. But a text doesn't help feed and bathe Reagan. We've talked about this."

"We also talked about how it doesn't make sense to keep Reagan in day care while you look for another job. We can't afford it."

"No, what we can't afford is to be inviting people over for a birthday party right now."

"Is that why you bought that ghetto piñata? To send a message?"

"I need you home by six. End of discussion."

"Well, that's not always possible."

"You need to make it possible. You know what, I'm going to talk to Dale. He needs to understand what's going on."

"Absolutely not. You're not talking to Dale."

"Why not? What are you so worried about? You afraid he'll reveal your little secret?"

"What are you talking about?"

"I know you're fucking him. All those times you've been late, I know what's going on."

"Jesus, this is ridiculous. All I ever do is complain about Dale. You think I want to have an affair with him? Of all people?"

"So there are other people you want to have an affair with."

"Listen to yourself. You're paranoid. I'm going to bed."

"Don't walk away when I'm talking to you."

"Give me a reason to stay and listen to this bullshit."

"Fucking bitch! You know better than to talk to me like that."

The next sound I heard was Mom sobbing as she walked upstairs and passed Reagan's bedroom. From below, Dad yelled "Two-minute rule." Like mother, like son.

"Happy birthday, baby," Mom said when she came to get Reagan out of bed the next morning.

"Mommy boo-boo," Reagan said.

"It's okay, sweetie. Mommy fell down."

"Daddy," he said, speaking from personal experience.

Mom dodged the implication. "Are you excited about your party?" She turned toward me and I saw her "boo-boo," a purple half-circle under her right eye.

"Two," Reagan said.

"That's right. You're two years old. Such a big boy."

She changed Reagan out of his pajamas, noticing his own set of bruises from the day before. I waited for her to say something, to explode in a fit of rage at her husband for laying a hand on their defenseless son. Instead, she finished getting Reagan dressed and carried both of us downstairs, setting us both on the kitchen counter, me facedown.

"Wanna help Mommy put candy in the piñata?"

"Yeah."

Mom pressed on my back and I felt part of me lift, followed by the crinkling of bags being opened. I was filling up with candy and uncertainty, though Reagan's obvious pleasure helped ease my anxiety. They finished, closed me and stood me back up, the candy sliding down and settling in my lower half. It was strange to feel full, like I had been missing a vital part of my essence until now. I was still unclear why they'd want to store candy inside me, but Reagan had taken such good care of me so far that I knew I was safe with him.

Dad tied a knot above my head and threw the rope over a tree branch. He raised me up until my head almost touched the tree and then wrapped the excess rope around the branch. This would be my vantage point for the day. I wasn't sure why I was up there, but it was wonderful, a tremendous view.

Before the guests arrived, Mom covered her bruise with makeup. Dad made sure he had a beer in his hand at all times. Reagan ran around the backyard with the other kids, Dad reminding him to keep it down if he thought Reagan got too excited. Seeing Reagan smile and laugh and play filled up my top half with as much weight as my bottom half now held. I watched them eat lunch and listened to a rousing birthday song that was topped off with cake.

I couldn't help but notice that Dad had been on his best behavior all day. Maybe yesterday was just a fluke, a bad day, the stress of being a husband and father getting the better of him. The guests at the party seemed to like him well enough; I even saw him smile when Reagan's face was coated with frosting.

"Piñata time, everybody," Dad shouted.

The kids gathered around the tree, shoving each other a little to secure a good spot. I was on display and hoped that I looked as good as I felt. I got the impression that my whole life had been leading up to this moment, a sense of fulfillment washing over me. Everyone was staring at me. Now if only I knew what they were expecting me to do.

"Reagan, you're first," Dad said.

Reagan ran up to Dad, who put a blindfold on him and handed him a baseball bat. Reagan took a quick swing, barely missing Dad's leg. Was this payback for what Dad had done to him? It seemed odd to exact revenge in front of friends and family, but however Dad got his come-uppance was fine with me.

"Hang on. Not yet," Dad said. He unwrapped the rope I was hanging from and lowered me halfway to the ground. "Okay, go."

Reagan swung again, narrowly missing my legs this time as Dad yanked me up. Whew, that was close. The crowd oohed. Another swing, another miss, the candy inside me moving around, the weight making me sway. Was it just me or were these swings coming closer to me than they were Dad? Someone needed to take that blindfold off, so Reagan could see his target more clearly.

Dad lowered me again as Mom came over to direct Reagan, pointing him straight at me.

"Swing hard, sweetie," she told him, and I finally understood that Dad wasn't the mark after all. My gut instinct from the start had been that these people hated me, but I had convinced myself otherwise. Then again, given Dad's proclivity for violence, maybe this was just how they expressed love. Trying to hit me with a bat might be their greatest show of affection.

Reagan swung one more time, connecting with my legs, sending me in circles. Cheers erupted from the party-goers. Dad steadied me before calling out for the next kid to take a turn. Apparently, they all hated me, even the ones I didn't know. There was a mob mentality here — the people versus Elmo.

Whack!

The next kid was bigger than Reagan. They even spun him around a few times before he swung, and he still managed to hit me twice.

Bam!

That one landed right in my stomach, and again, I was going in circles.

Pow!

Three more kids took their shots at me before Reagan's turn came back around. I felt a looseness in my legs.

"Hold the rope," Dad said to Mom. "Come here, Reagan."

"Just let the kids do it," Mom said.

"We're gonna finish this thing." Dad gripped the bat with Reagan. "You ready, buddy?"

"Yeah."

They swung hard, tearing off my right leg and leaving a dent in my stomach that rivaled the one I already had in my head. Dad's eyes meant business. Whatever they were doing this for, this was going to be the blow that would end it.

Blam!

My insides ripped open and the candy Mom and Reagan had put inside spilled to the ground. The kids rushed under me, frantic to pick the stuff up. One of them, seeing that some of the candy hadn't dropped, pulled my bottom half, which was barely hanging on, away from the rest of me. Mom lowered what was left of me to the ground, where I had a better view of the scavengers who had each played a part in my body's desecration.

I thought back to the other piñatas at the party supply store. I wondered if they would meet the same fate as me, if this was the only reason we existed, a parent-approved vessel for kids to vent their rage in the name of fun and end up with a candy reward when the beating was done. It occurred to me that I may not have suffered as much as others. At least half of me escaped relatively unscathed.

"All right, let's go inside and watch Reagan open his presents," Mom said when all the candy had been collected.

The crowd dispersed, except for Dad, who started cleaning up my broken parts.

For a second I thought that he might try to put me back together so they could have another go at me. He gathered all my pieces and cradled them in one arm.

Mom came back outside. "Hey, Reagan's waiting for you. Leave that for later."

"Start without me. Tell him I'll be there in a minute."

She kissed him, the first sign of warmth I'd seen between them since I arrived. "Okay."

"And you might want to touch that up," he said, pointing at her bruise.

The reminder deflated her. "Thanks," she said, and went back inside.

With his free hand, Dad took the lid off a trash can and dumped me in. He made multiple trips, dropping off plates, cups, aluminum cans. Before long, I was covered in potato salad and cake and soda. He put the lid back on the trash can. My new home.

# NON-FICTION

# Blown Away:
# Paul B. Sears and Oklahoma

*Michael Snyder*

Inside the Sam Noble Museum of Natural History in Norman, Oklahoma, one finds a large inscription on the wall near the imposing bronze sculpture of a tusked wooly mammoth and a prehistoric hunter. It is a profound quotation, one that encourages a cosmic perspective:

> *The face of the earth is a graveyard and so it has always been . . . each living thing restores when it dies that which has been borrowed, to give form and substance to its brief day in the sun. What is lent earth has been used by countless generations of plants and animals now dead, and will be required by countless others in the future.*
> –Paul B. Sears

That kind of puts things in perspective, doesn't it? We are part of a grand continuum, a tiny part of nature's endless cycle of life, death, and rebirth. We glory in our brief day in the sun, which too soon passes. Nothing lasts, but at least in some sense we are a part of continuing life. And we can endeavor to make the most of our transitory existence and "live deep and suck the very marrow of life," as Thoreau wrote. It's depressing yet inspiring at the same time.

Usually one would expect the words of an Aristotle, Charles Darwin, or Rachel Carson engraved on the wall of such an esteemed institution. So who was Paul B. Sears? Why are his words enshrined in the halls of the grand Sam Noble Museum? Though his name is not well known today, we owe him a debt of gratitude, and would do well to return to his teachings.

Paul Bigelow Sears was a prominent botanist and conservationist who, like my own ancestors, grew up on a farm in Ohio. He taught at the University of Oklahoma for a decade (1928-1938) and chaired its Botany department. In 1935, Sears published his signature work, *Deserts on the March,* with the University of Oklahoma Press while he was a professor there. A landmark work, it was one of the earliest books to convey ecological principles to the general reading public and to address the pressing dilemma of the Dust Bowl and its causes. It sold well for a book by a scientist. Its first chapter's opening lines furnish the quotation engraved at the Sam Noble Museum.

Paul Sears composed *Deserts of the March* in Oklahoma during the early part of the Dust Bowl, when gloomy walls of dust combined with the Great Depression to form a profound sense of futility and dread.

In the book, he made recommendations to avoid such disasters in the future. He went beyond writing in his efforts. During the 1930s, Sears chaired an advisory committee examining the Dust Bowl in Oklahoma, which drafted a soil conservation district law. Sears urged mandatory soil conservation methods including planting wheat fields with cover crops and native grasses. These efforts made a real difference.

*Deserts on the March* is important for its influence and historical value, but, unusual for a work by a scientist, it's also a great work of literature that draws from history, philosophy, and psychology along with Sears's fields of expertise. It's absolutely worth reading today. Along with the University of Oklahoma, Sears also taught at Ohio State University, University of Nebraska, Oberlin College, and Yale, where his papers are archived, and he published a handful of books, including a study of Darwin. Everywhere he worked, he created conservation programs and materials on ecology for teachers and students of science. He was a one-man crusade brimming over with energy. He got stuff done.

Sears understood that science can only go so far in solving the problems that face humankind. He stressed that an ecologist, along with scientific knowledge, should also possess great communication skills to reach the farmer, the landowner, the hunter, and the politician. Thus, elsewhere on the walls of the Sam Noble Museum, another quotation from *Deserts on the March* is inscribed:

> Science has the power to illuminate, but not to solve, the deeper problems of mankind. For always after knowledge come choice and action, both of them intensely personal.

To catalyze personal action, Sears knew he had to reach the people, not just other scientists and professors. His publisher and friend, Joseph A. Brandt, Director of the University of Oklahoma Press, who went on to become to President of the University of Oklahoma, remarked: "Paul Sears knew the people, he liked them, and he associated with them. And he knew how to write for them ... the people read the book and took it to heart. Something was done about the Dust Bowl." *Deserts on the March* therefore is a marvelous example of rhetoric, in that the power of knowledge and conviction are empowered by great writing to reach people and inspire them to act.

Publishing and speaking with people of various levels of society, Paul Sears spread a message that we still need to hear today. Nature is indifferent to humankind, but we must be stewards of it, fighting soil erosion. Water is a precious, indispensable resource. We must work together to conserve our natural commonwealth. We must think communally, modeling ourselves on indigenous practices. Wasteful and exploitative methods that profit individuals but deplete resources and harm the land must be stopped. What he wrote in the 1930s remains relevant, echoed by contemporary writers such as Barbara Kingsolver in her essay "Water is Life," collected in *Water Matters*. Sears noted that much of what he was recommending had in essence been advised since the ancient Greek poet Hesiod's *Works and Days*. The question is, will we listen and act?

Paul Sears was a good friend to the mixed-blood Osage author John Joseph Mathews, who also published with OU Press. Sears, Mathews, George Milburn, Stanley Vestal (Walter S. Campbell), Joseph Brandt, and others formed an Oklahoman literary and publishing scene that prized the great outdoors and embraced ecological concepts. Sears taught "Jo" Mathews about ecology from a scientific point of view and Mathews taught Sears about ecology from an indigenous Osage perspective. Sears was a repeat visitor to the Blackjacks, the stone home that Mathews built out on the prairie ridge on his family's Osage allotment land on the Osage Nation. They sipped liquor and swapped stories of animals and nature through the evening. In his book *Talking to the Moon*, which largely focuses on observations of his prairie environment, Mathews describes a tree that seemed to grow "on a flat sandstone rock without visible soil support." Every time he looked at it, he felt that "Paul Sears, famed botanist and friend, should be here to appreciate it with me."

Friends like John Joseph Mathews helped to spread Paul Sears's ecological message. Mathews brought several copies of *Deserts on the March* to Washington, DC on his trips on behalf of the Osage Tribal Council, and gave them to Congressmen such as the mighty Senator Thomas P. Gore of Oklahoma (author Gore Vidal's grandfather and early mentor), and other prominent men in the capital. Sears visited the Blackjacks during the springs of 1936 and 1937 and exchanged several letters with Mathews, especially during the late 1930s and 1940s. In 1937, Mathews invited Sears and Joe Brandt out to the Blackjacks to observe the prairie chickens dancing and he noted that his friend, Oklahoma fiction writer George Milburn (*Oklahoma Town*) and his wife Vivien had been visiting. Later, Paul wrote to Mathews in a letter archived at Yale: "We all had a grand time and came back rested and refreshed. We needed all of this accumulated energy, however, to withstand the onslaught of our better halves when they found out that we had really gone nearly 200 miles to watch prairie chickens dance." He joked, "The next time I think we shall have to select some less innocent objective to maintain our prestige."

One thing that Mathews no doubt appreciated about Sears was his sympathy for Native American perspectives. He stressed that the white man ought to have commingled, consulted with, and learned from the indigenous experts on the land, but instead engaged in agricultural practices that demonstrated their lack of deep knowledge of the terrain, with sometimes dreadful results. In *Deserts on the March*, Sears has some sharp words for the assumptions and justifications of white settler colonialism. He notes that American settlers brought their women and resisted intermarrying with Native women. The presence of womenfolk "provided a certain sanction for every aggressive move against the aborigines. One of the most significant traits of Anglo-Saxon psychology is the need for lofty motives during the process of getting whatever may be wanted. More a capacity for self-deception than a matter of perfidy or hypocrisy, it nevertheless lies at the root of much of the mischief done to the resources of the North American continent." This is a piercing indictment of Euro-American illusions and the justification of violence and expropriation. The settler and farmer moved across the West, destroying Native culture as he went, stressing at every mile "individual property rights in the land without regard for public policy." Sears boldly questions the rights of individual landowners to follow practices that are harmful to the collective good. His more socialistic ideas and criticism of unfettered capitalism may have been one reason why he published only one book during the anti-communist hysteria of the 1940s and 1950s.

The Dust Bowl was the inevitable consequence of white greed and lack of harmony with the land. Sears writes: "Mile-high, these gloomy curtains of dust were the proper backdrops for the tragedy that was on the boards. The lustful march of the white race across the virgin continent, strewn with ruined forests, polluted streams, gullied fields, stained by the breaking of treaties and titanic greed, can no longer be disguised behind the camouflage that we call civilization." Rarely does one find such a sharp and perceptive critique from non-Native scientists and scholars, couched in such poetic yet accessible language. These sentiments were mirrored by his friend John Joseph Mathews.

*Deserts on the March* has been republished in new editions multiple times. Given the environmental crises we face, largely resulting from our species' short-sightedness and pursuit of individual profit over the communal good, perhaps we need to heed the wise words of Paul Sears once again. He understood that science must form a bridge with psychology and its knowledge must be expressed in clear, appealing language to reach the people if it is to be put into practice and its benefits enjoyed. As he stated, *"It is not merely soil, nor plant, nor animal, nor weather that we need to know better, but chiefly man himself."*

# When Bouncing Bettys
# and Truth Collide

*Brenden Stovall*

*In the end, of course, a true war story is never about war. It's about
the special way that dawn spreads out on a river when you know you
must cross the river and march into the mountains and do things
you are afraid to do. It's about love and memory. It's about sorry.
It's about sisters who never write back and people who never listen.*
                                                          –Tim O'Brien

What constitutes a good war story? I suppose it depends upon the context
and the moment. Sometimes, though, you hear a war story so outrageous,
so farfetched and unbelievable, it might as well be part of a fantasy novel.
If you believe a story like that, then yes, Jedi do exist, my farts do smell
like roses, and Iraq will someday be a peaceful, fertile nation.

I heard such a tale from a young soldier while engaged in pre-de-
ployment training at Fort Stewart, Georgia, back in 2007. We were going
through STX lanes (a series of miniature courses where soldiers learn a
variety of skills necessary for combat). The particular station where I met
this young man involved learning the proper techniques for searching
dead bodies on the ground and live persons under detainment. He played
the role of guinea pig for the crotch swab technique — you know, where
you feel around the upper-inner part of the pant leg and up into the crack,
a move also known as the credit card swipe. He followed Rivera and me
over to the smoke pit during a ten-minute break.

We stood talking, like guys do, about Iraq and girls and the endless
list of things we would rather be doing. This guy, a Specialist no older
than twenty-one, was goofy looking. His right eye cocked lazily to the
right. As we smoked, Rivera and I stood side-by-side wondering which
one of us he was looking at. He bummed a cigarette, and upon overhear-
ing us comment on how we felt that the training was bullshit, decided
he would school us.

"Take the training seriously," said the Specialist. "It could save
your life."

Rivera and I exchanged casual glances of amusement. "Okay, dude,"
Rivera said. "It sucks that you have to be molested all day."

"It's serious training," said the Specialist. "I volunteered for this."

I rolled my eyes. Nobody volunteers for that. Nobody. Rivera started
sounding off. "Dude, you didn't volunteer for that. You're a fucking

specialist," he said, pointing at his rank. "Why aren't you with your unit getting ready to deploy?" At that I looked at Rivera, my expression saying, *Dude, leave him alone, he's just a dipshit. He can't help it.* Rivera countered with a look of, I don't care.

"Because I'm too valuable to the training," Cockeye returned, his tone as serious as his expression. A true believer, this guy. "They need me here," he said.

"Yeah, you're that hardcore, huh?" I said.

It is common knowledge in the infantry world that if your unit is deploying and you aren't, something is up — especially if you are only a young soldier. This was Third Infantry Division, and it deployed every other year from 2002-2011. Fact is, you had to be pretty screwed up to be left behind. "I'm serious. You guys need to take this training seriously," he insisted.

I pointed at the combat patch on my right shoulder. "Hey, kid, I've fucking deployed before. I don't know what you think you know that I don't."

He studied me for a moment, or maybe it was Rivera, hard to tell with those crazy eyes. Then he broke out into the story of all war stories, the ultimate one-upper before I could even fully initiate the contest.

"On my last deployment, we were out on patrol. We stopped on a dirt route, dismounted, and began walking around because we were bored. It was hot outside, like one-fifty." (Disclaimer: He's the only Joe I've ever met brave enough to claim 150 degree weather in Iraq.) "While I was scanning my sector, a private was walking around. He was new, you know, curious. All of a sudden, I grabbed his shoulder and said, 'Don't move if you want to live.'"

Rivera started to walk away, his eyes rolling. I grabbed his arm, and said, "Don't move if you want to live." We cracked up.

"I'm serious," he said. "He was standing on a Bouncing Betty."

My head whipped around like a cartoon character's. "A fucking what?" I asked.

Rivera grabbed my shoulder. "Really? A Bouncing Betty in Iraq? Oh my God, what did you do?"

Ignoring the sarcasm in our voices, he continued. "I knew straight off it was pressure plated, so I told him, don't move. He stood there stiff, crying. I knew I had to act quickly, so I sprinted to my Humvee and grabbed the chains, hooked them to the back of the guy's vest. 'This is going to hurt,' I told him. I hooked the chains up to the back of my Humvee and slammed the gas, taking it to sixty miles per hour instantly. He was out of blast radius by the time the Bouncing Betty popped up and detonated."

"What the fuck, dude? Humvees don't go zero to sixty in — "

I cut Rivera off. "Was he hurt?" By that point, why not egg him on?

"Oh yeah, but he lived. I made a tourniquet out of my belt and shoe-laces for his leg. His shoulder was ripped out of socket by the force of the Humvee yanking him. But he lived."

"Which lane covers Bouncing Betties?" Rivera asked.

I've always appreciated that story. I've heard a lot of lies and bullshit over the ten plus years of service, but never one that nears the "Don't move if you want to live" story, as we refer to it. I sit and think, what if I didn't smoke? I would've spent the rest of my life having never heard the greatest load of shit ever told. I imagine that even a civilian who knows nothing about Iraq or combat could call bullshit on that one. If you'll buy it, maybe he'll throw in a tale or two about POW camps in Kuwait where they torture soldiers with camel spiders for information. Maybe he'll tell you about the time he went to the USSR and when he returned a week later, it was called Russia.

His story is a good one. Seriously, I know it's an uphill argument, but that is a good war story. It's got action, heroism, and no important, tedious morals to contemplate on. There's nothing gross or inhumane about saving another man from a Vietnam-era booby trap with nothing but chains and a freakishly super-charged Humvee. It has the most important element of all: A happy ending. Everyone lives.

I've heard all varieties of war stories. I've told a few. I've told people that I deployed and came back alive. That's a good story. I've told people about walking in the villages and neighborhoods and factories in Iraq in full battle rattle. Maybe I lied. Maybe I didn't tell them the truth. Maybe I did get blown up over there, or maybe I shot a kid in the head, or maybe I never fired my weapon once, never even went on a patrol. If the listener wasn't there, they can only be a skeptic. A good war story is appropriate for the setting. But it shouldn't be a downer, should it?

Want to hear war stories for real? Want to get a clear picture of the blood and guts and glory? Get a Joe hammered at the bar. I mean, ine-briated. Tanked. Ask him a few questions. He'll slur a bit, get defensive, and say something like, "What's the point, what you want to know? Fuck that country." Just watch and wait while he sways in his bar stool, star-ing off into space. Feed him a few more shots. It'll evolve quickly into anger. "Fuck all of 'em, ya know." A fist might slam, his face beginning to twitch. Then, after a few minutes, it'll be a rant of confusion. "I don't understand, ya know, it's not fucking fair that he didn't make it and I did." From there it just becomes depressing. "It should've been me." He'll probably weep while drinking. If you get to that point, you're fucked, and now you get to hear a real war story and see the emotion behind it. Even though the story has an ending, it never ends, because he owns that story, it's alive within him every minute of every day. That story has no happy ending, therefore, no ending for the storyteller. What happened is unresolved, so it just stays with him.

Real war stories are only fun if they're fond memories. Like the time we pulled a prank on Shartzer by dumping powdered drink down his throat while he was sleeping, or making fun of Johnson because he used an empty juice carton as a masturbation tool. (He cut a hole in the bottom and stuffed it with tissue. Ride 'em, cowboy.)

The stories that aren't fun are the bad ones, because there's no punchline associated with remembering the smell of dead flesh or the concussion of an IED. Who wants to hear about that? The people that have those stories hold them close to the chest, like a disease they don't want to share. That pain is an infection. Sharing stories like that gets nothing but uncomfortable silences and pity. No respectable person wants pity.

The problem is that the Joes are geared immediately for the pursuit of 'Real War Stories.' They come in green at eighteen or nineteen out of basic training and they can't wait to deploy, to see the shit, earn their wings, so to speak, by getting their own story. They don't understand why the sergeants are assholes about it, why they don't talk about the shit unless they're drunk. Those young bucks aren't afraid of dying or getting hurt. They are afraid of coming back from deployment without the scars. That's a true story. Your trip to the sandbox isn't legit without hardship, without experiencing some real shit. The Joe feels guilty without the bad story.

A true war story exposes the truth, but sometimes the truth shouldn't be told. When our platoon sergeant died, a Joe from the medical battalion assisted with removing the body from the vehicle, and then a day or two later proceeded to tell everyone how bad it was. He told people about how the body was in pieces, how it looked to piece him back together at mortuary affairs. It was upsetting people in our outfit because we knew the man and loved him. Almost everyone in the company wasn't there when it happened and didn't know — or need to know — what it looked and smelled like. This medic never knew our friend, so it didn't bother him. He wore that experience on his chest like a medal. He finally shut his mouth when I almost knocked his teeth out.

Or maybe I didn't. Maybe that isn't a true war story, just a tale to get my point across. With a war story you never really know what is true or what isn't unless you were there. It is important to remember, though, that most of the time some part of the story is true. Maybe it wasn't me that threatened the soldier and told his supervisor. Maybe it was Sergeant Brock. Maybe Sergeant Brock stopped me from beating the soldier half to death, and decided to take the issue to the supervisor himself. Perhaps neither of us did a damn thing. There is, no matter how you shake it, still some truth. One — or some — variation is true.

One problem with war stories is coming home without one. When you are there and a kid is killed, you have that story you can't shake. When your friend is the one with that story, it's easy to feel the guilt of not having been there to share it. To know your brothers are out there getting lit up while you had the night off is tough. Most Joes would rather be hit than have someone else get hit. Like when Hartley died. Some were there, some weren't, but there wasn't a man among us who didn't wish it had been us and not him. Some of us dealt with seeing his body at casualty affairs, some dealt with pulling wounded soldiers out of the vehicle. Most didn't. Maybe I was there, maybe I wasn't. Some variation is true, though, because Hartley did die, he did go to casualty affairs, he was sent home in a box. Not a good war story at all.

Coming home without a story, a scar, can be painful. After we returned from Iraq we got a new chaplain in the unit. He counseled a soldier one time, and I asked the chaplain afterward, "How is he?"

"He's upset, having a hard time."

"'Bout what?"

"What he saw when Hartley died."

"What the fuck? He wasn't fucking there when Hartley died."

"How do you know?"

My story was none of that chaplain's business. But I knew Specialist Pants on Fire wasn't there. I told the chaplain that Specialist Pity Party was full of the devil's juice and needed some Ten Commandment healing.

Then again, maybe we all really were there the day he died, and for all the other KIAs as well. The guilt of not being there when it happened is real, is painful. Just losing someone you know or care about is difficult enough on its own. Maybe carrying the story of not being there is so hard that you imagine and fantasize sharing that fucked up experience, not to impress your parents or girlfriends, but to feel less guilty. It could be that's where these good war stories come from, too. Then to make the story a better one, change the names of the soldiers in the story to preserve their dignity. Don't actually rat them out for being flawed.

Want to hear a good, true war story? I have a friend who deployed with the National Guard for nine months in Iraq. He came home uninjured and so did the rest of his unit. No one killed in action, no one wounded. They trained, they went, they returned. All of them. Damn good story.

It could be that Specialist Bouncing Betty was smarter than we thought he was. Maybe his story is real, just with an unhappy ending. Perhaps the Joe he claims to have saved got blown all over the road by an IED. It's possible that he wishes every day he could have done something to change the outcome. Maybe there really is a reason he takes that training so serious, and maybe there's a legitimate reason he wasn't deploying with his unit and was happy to be molested by every Joe coming through his lane before their deployment. Maybe fiction is better than truth, and perhaps a happy ending, regardless of how out-of-this-world it may seem, is just what is needed during a ten minute smoke break before getting back to training for combat.

The truth is that Specialist Molest-Me gave me a story to share a laugh over. In the end, regardless of whether the Bouncing Betty story is a lie, or my stories are true, they still share a distinctive trait. All the stories, fact or fiction, truth or lie, are still, in the end, just stories. That's the real truth.

# Squirrel on the Roof

## Francis DiClemente

The squirrel refused to be intimidated by my figure appearing in the window.

I was spending a few days with my stepfather, Bill, at his home in Rome, New York, during the week of Christmas 2013. One afternoon, I went upstairs to grab one of my prescriptions from the guest bedroom.

I paused on the landing leading to the upper floor and gazed out the window. Thin white clouds slid across a blue sky more suited for June than December. Bright sunlight radiated against the layer of snow that covered the backyard, and the tall pine trees standing in the alley behind Bill's house swayed in the breeze.

I saw the brown squirrel running on the roof of the addition to the house — which included the family room and a small mudroom located at the back entrance. Tiny squirrel tracks dotted the snow on the roof and led to an ash tree with large branches leaning over the house.

This squirrel sat up on his hind legs with his front paws pressed to his mouth as he nibbled on a seed or a small nut. He was turned in profile to me, so the left side of his head and body faced me. He had grayish-brown fur with fine hairs and small black eyes.

The squirrel seemed to be looking at me out of the corner of his eye. I tapped loudly on the window and said, "Hey, hey, get outta there. Get off there."

I was worried he would sneak into the house, either by going down the chimney or squeezing through an opening somewhere on the roof.

But the squirrel remained in place near the window. I banged on the glass again.

He ran a few feet away and then stopped. He scurried back to his original spot and resumed eating his morsel while continuing to look at me out of the corner of his eye. He had judged correctly that I was unwilling to crawl out on the roof and chase him away.

I considered opening the window, reaching down to make a snowball and tossing it at the squirrel. But I feared if I lifted the storm window, the squirrel would leap past me and enter the house.

I imagined the scratching sound his claws would make on the hardwood staircase if he got inside and ran downstairs. I thought about the shock Bill would receive if he saw the squirrel racing around the kitchen or family room.

I knocked on the glass again, waved my hands and yelled at the squirrel, attempting to shoo him away. He ignored my gesticulations and stood his ground.

Then I conjured an image of the animal in human form, taking on the shape, appearance and personality of a tough-guy New York City construction worker, a sarcastic pragmatist.

I imagined if the squirrel could have talked at that moment, he would have said to me: "Go ahead buddy. Bang all you want. I'm not going anywhere. Sure, open the window if you want. I'll be in that house so fast you won't know where to find me. I'll crawl into your bed and gnaw on your face at night."

"So get this — I'm staying put. You have your living space and we have ours. I'm not bothering you and you're not gonna push me around. Plus you're too afraid. You don't have the stones to open the window and force me to leave."

After the imaginary, one-way conversation, I decided it was unnecessary to waste any more time worrying about the squirrel. I figured if he could have found a way to sneak into the house via the roof, he would have done so already.

I moved away from the landing, walking up the last few steps of the staircase and then entered my guest bedroom. I grabbed the pill I needed from the top of the dresser and headed back downstairs. I did not look outside as I passed in front of the window again, as I avoided the alert black eyes of the squirrel. But I suspected the animal was still crouched on the roof, eating his nut, confident that his meal would no longer be disrupted and his home would remain secure.

POSTSCRIPT: SUMMER 2014

The following summer the homeowner took action to address the squirrel infestation. Bill decided he was fed up with acorns being scattered on his patio and the squirrels stealing all of the birdseed from his bird feeder. He bought some metal cages, put peanuts in them and placed the traps on the back lawn, near the bird feeder.

Bill owns and operates a small contracting company in Rome. He and Butch, one of his laborers, would set the traps repeatedly, and over the course of the summer they nabbed 18 squirrels (at last count).

They also developed a strategy for removing the rodents. At first, Butch would release them in the neighborhood, but then Bill and Butch discovered that some of them had returned to the backyard. They knew this because Butch had sprayed the tail of one of the squirrels with yellow parking lot line paint; he let it go a few blocks away from Bill's house, near the Rome Art and Community Center. And sure enough the squirrel came back again, scampering freely in the yard with a streak of yellow color showing on its back end.

From that point on, Bill and Butch transported the squirrels to an area near Delta Lake dam in the Town of Western, north of Rome.

The backyard is much quieter now. When I visit Bill I rarely see squirrels darting about on the lawn, racing up the trunks of the trees or hanging off the bird feeder, stealing the birdseed from Bill's feathered neighbors. I also wonder if Bill and Butch captured my rebellious friend, or if the rodent in question avoided the temptation of the peanuts and escaped the jaws of the metal cage. I'd like to think the squirrel I observed on the roof is now enjoying a new home near the dense forestland surrounding Delta Lake.

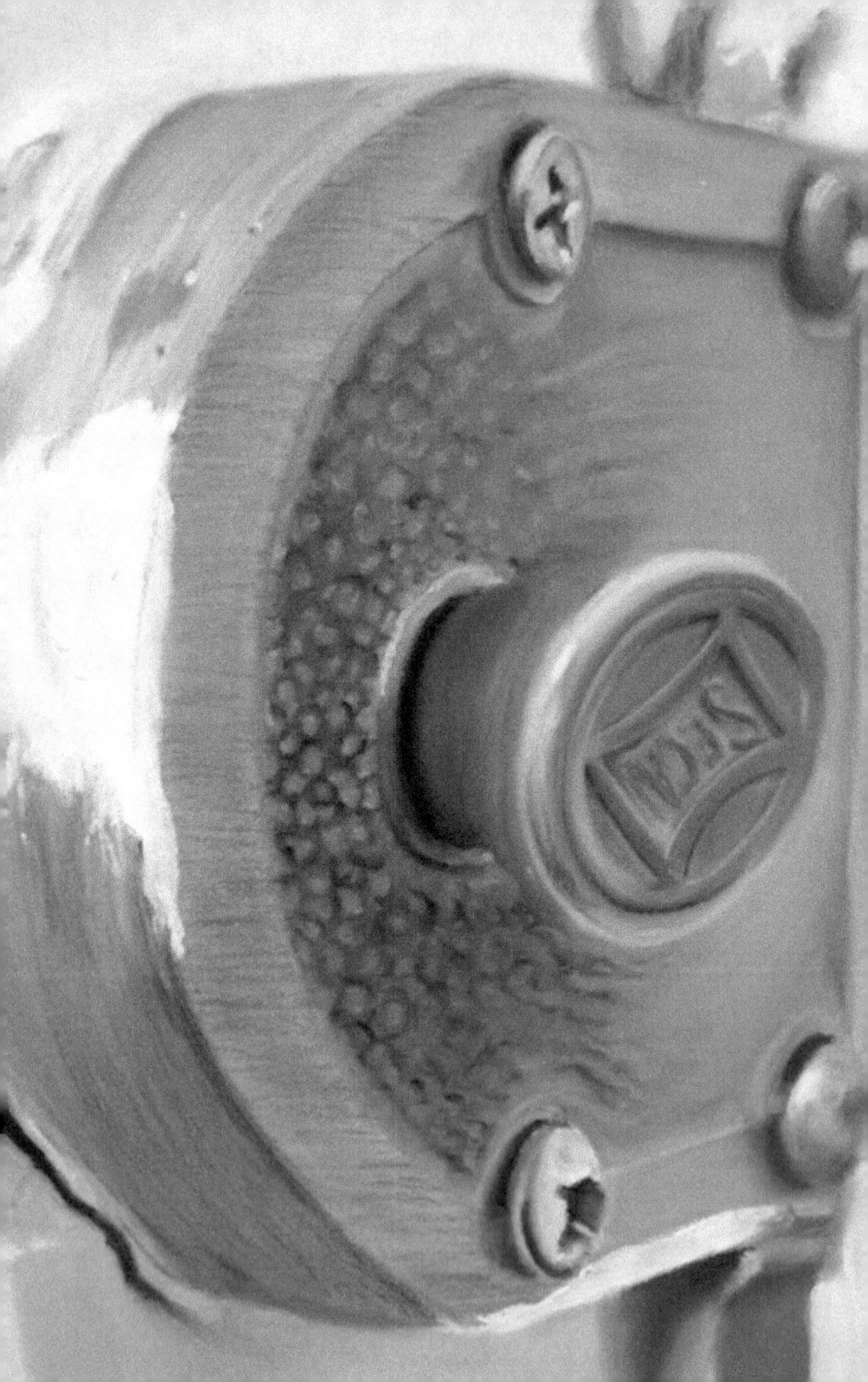

# ABOUT THE
# CONTRIBUTORS

# Poetry

### Jon Ballard

Jon Ballard is the author of one novel, *Year of the Poets* (Loose Leaves Publications, 2014), and five poetry chapbooks, including most recently *Somewhere Between* (Finishing Line Press, 2014). His work has appeared in *Cimarron Review, Flint Hills Review, Valparaiso Poetry Review, Oklahoma Review,* and *Broadsided.* He is an adjunct writing instructor at Oakland Community College in southeastern Michigan.

### Seth Benton

Seth Benton lives in Williamsburg, Virginia, with his wife and son. His poems have recently appeared in *Sheepshead Review, Roanoke Review, Cold Mountain Review,* and *Common Ground Review.*

### Paul Bernstein

Paul Bernstein is a retired medical editor and self-taught poet whose recent work has appeared in *Front Porch Review, Big River Poetry Journal, River Poets Review, Poetry Quarterly, U.S. 1 Worksheets,* and elsewhere. He is also a prizewinning amateur country music lyricist. Paul currently lives in Ann Arbor, Michigan, where he participates regularly in open mic readings.

### Mark Burke

Mark Burke is a graduate of the Pacific University MFA program. His work has been published or is forthcoming in the *Beloit Poetry Journal, Southern Humanities Review, Sugar House Review,* and other magazines.

### Kaycee Chance

Kaycee Chance is a graduate student at the University of Central Oklahoma, where she also works as a Composition instructor. Although she is currently focusing on her first complete collection of poetry, she is also working on several short stories and a novel. She is a firm believer that there is nothing a good outfit, thunderstorm, cup of coffee, or random fit of laughter can't fix. When she is not writing, you can find her reading, listening to music, gardening, walking her dog, snuggling her four cats, or binge-watching Netflix with her husband.

### Addison Eaton

Addison Eaton is a twenty-something poet working on her second master's degree. She is an elementary school librarian, sweet tea aficionado, champion of renegade causes that involve glitter, and mother to an overweight corgi named Gatsby. When she isn't saving the world in Broken Arrow, Oklahoma, or scowling in dark corners of bars, she's moonlighting as a butcher, baker, and candlestick maker. This is her second time to be published in the *New Plains Review*. Parts of this bio may or may not be true.

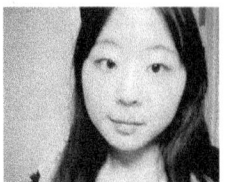

### Taehyun Han

Taehyun Han came to the United States from South Korea in 2014 to pursue her bachelor's degree in Creative Writing at the University of Central Oklahoma. She thanks her family and friends for their love and support of her journey. Her poem, "Daily Life," was composed when she had her first panic attack; right after the attack, she found the poem drilled into her head, replacing the deadly dread she'd just gone through. Following one word after another, she made her way out of the fear.

### Michael Constantine McConnell

Michael Constantine McConnell's poetry and prose have been featured in such anthologies as *The Best of Electric Velocipede, Body and Soul: Narratives of Healing from Ars Medica, Reading Lips and Other Ways to Overcome a Disability,* and *Solace in So Many Words,* for which he was nominated for a 2011 Pushcart Prize in the essay category. Originally from Detroit, he is currently a proud resident of San Marcos, Texas, where he is pursuing a doctoral degree in Developmental Education at Texas State University and singing in degenerate Scots-Irish bands after sundown.

### Steve Nickman

Steve Nickman lives in Brookline, Massachusetts and takes part in the Workshop for Publishing Poets. He is a psychiatrist and works mainly with kids, teenagers, and young adults. He has a strong interest in the experiences and dilemmas of adoptees and their families, and is working on a book about therapy, *The Wound and the Spark.* Steve's poetry is forthcoming or has recently appeared in *Cape Cod Poetry Review, Third Wednesday, Rhino Magazine, Mid-American Review,* and *Antigonish Review.*

## Neelanjana Shakya

Neelanjana Shakya is a confused 23 year old. She published a book of poems titled *Netted Shadows* while in Nigeria at the age of 17. She is a socially awkward person and enjoys music and magic.

## Amie Sharp

Amie Sharp's work has appeared or is forthcoming in *Atticus Review, Badlands,* the *Bellevue Literary Review, Forge, Lascaux Review,* and the *Saint Katherine Review,* among others. A native of Tennessee, she received an MA in English from the University of South Florida and an MFA in poetry from Seattle Pacific University. She's a member of the Colorado Poets Center and assistant professor of English at Pikes Peak Community College.

## Sam Herschel Wein

Sam Wein is a graduate of Washington University in St. Louis who currently resides in Chicago. He has been a fellow at Tent: Creative Writing for Nonfiction in Amherst, Massachusetts, and is currently the editorial assistant at *Construction Magazine.* His work has appeared previously in *Mobius Magazine, a Journal for Social Change.*

# Visual Art

### Elizabeth Brown

Elizabeth Brown is an artist from a cross-disciplinary background of printmaking and fibers. Drawn to the study of form and structure in organisms her current work is focused on mixed media sculpture that investigates the inherent qualities and limitations of synthetic materials. This study between surface and structure creates small, intimate work that resembles biological forms. Elizabeth received her BFA in Printmaking from the Rhode Island School of Design with an intensive year studying in Rome, Italy. She received her MFA in Fiber from Arizona State University. Her work has been exhibited in New York, Cincinnati, Phoenix, Washington and Oklahoma City. She is a Professor of Art at the University of Central Oklahoma.

### Ariana Foote

Ariana Foote is a painter, printmaker, and video artist living and working in Oklahoma City. She received her BFA in 2010 from the University of Central Oklahoma, and her MFA from Brooklyn College in 2014. Ariana has exhibited locally and nationally, and has taught at both the University of Central Oklahoma and Oklahoma City Community College.

### Allen Forrest

Graphic artist and painter Allen Forrest was born in Canada and bred in the US. He has created cover art and illustrations for literary publications and books. He is the winner of the Leslie Jacoby Honor for Art at San Jose State University's *Reed Magazine* and his Bel Red painting series is part of the Bellevue College Foundation's permanent art collection. Forrest's expressive drawing and painting style is a mix of avant-garde expressionism and post-impressionist elements reminiscent of van Gogh, creating emotion on canvas.

### Joshua Garrett

Joshua Garrett is a self-taught artist. He lives in Edmond, Oklahoma. More of his work can be seen at the Jacobson House Native American Art Gallery in Norman, Oklahoma.

## Michael Litzau

Michael received his Bachelor of Fine Arts in 2004 from Columbus College of Art and Design and in 2006 obtained his Master of Fine Arts degree at The Ohio State University in printmaking. The materials he uses often include scrapbook paper, wall paper, intaglio, and graphite. Together, the images and materials explore issues of craft and ritual. He is currently an Assistant Professor of Drawing at The University of Central Oklahoma where he over sees the drawing and printmaking area. Michael has shown his artwork extensively through solo, juried and trade print exhibitions throughout the United States.

## Scott Reno

Scott Reno is an Oklahoma born and raised professional golf instructor with a natural talent for portrait and wildlife art. A graduate of UCO in Edmond in 1980 with a degree in Business Finance, Scott now lives near Wagoner, OK, on property overlooking Fort Gibson Lake along with his wife Ginger and their 11 year old rescue German Shepherd dog named Kona. Most of Scott's time is spent helping students improve their golf game as well as coaching the Bixby Jr. High and High School golf teams. He has a passion for really good, slow smoked BBQ, as well as great home-cooked fried chicken and has been on a culinary quest to create his own irresistible versions of each.

## Jessica Scott

Jessica Scott is an independent photographer from Oklahoma City. When she's not taking pictures and attending Red Dirt Poetry events in Oklahoma City, she's playing Legend of Zelda or watching horror movies.

## Una Belle Townsend

Una Belle Townsend is an award winning children's author and a former teacher and librarian. She enjoys photography and writing children's books and poetry. She has received writing awards from the Oklahoma Center for the Book, the International Reading Assn./ Children's Choice Awards, and the Oklahoma Writer's Federation, Inc. Her latest book, *Sunsets and Haiku* is a blend of her photographs and descriptive haiku. *Sunsets and Haiku* will be available around Christmas. It is published by Doodle and Peck Publishing. She also has 3 other books coming out next year.

# Fiction

### Michael P. Adams

Michael P. Adams is a native Californian and a graduate of San Jose State University's MFA program. His fiction has appeared or is forthcoming in *Reed Magazine, Cardinal Sins, Crab Fat, Nomadic Journal, Dirty Chai,* and *Mosaic Art and Literary Journal.*

### Gary A. Berg

Gary A. Berg, MFA (UCLA) is the author of short stories and eight non-fiction books. His fiction has appeared in numerous publications including Euphemism, *The Summerset Review,* Santa Fe Writer's *Project, Synchronized Chaos, Cheap Pop, Vending Machine Press,* and *Work Literary Magazine.*

### Michael Cuglietta

Michael Cuglietta is a Florida writer. His work has appeared in *NOON, The Gettysburg Review, Tampa Review,* and *Passages North.* He is the author of the chapbook, *Vertigo* (Gertrude Press, 2014).

### Kirie C. Pedersen

Kirie C. Pedersen lives on the saltwater fjord of Hood Canal in Washington State. She holds a MA in literature and fiction writing. Her writing appears in literary magazines and journals, many linked to her blog at www. kiriepedersen.com.

### Tara Isabel Zambrano

Tara Isabel Zambrano lives in Texas with her husband and two kids. She moved from India to the United States two decades ago and is an electrical engineer by profession. Her work has been or will be published in *Isthmus, Redactions, SmokeLong Quarterly, Chiron Review, Bop Dead City,* and others.

# Non-fiction

**Francis DiClemente**

Francis DiClemente is a video producer and freelance writer who lives in Syracuse, New York. He is the author of three poetry chapbooks and his blog can be found at francisdiclemente.wordpress.com.

**Brenden Stovall**

Brenden Stovall is a former active duty soldier in the Army with over a decade of service. He is currently a Creative Writing major at the University of Central Oklahoma.

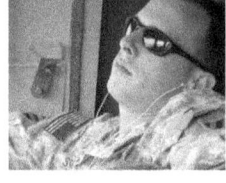

**Michael Snyder**

Michael Snyder will publish *I am Indigenous: The Life of Osage Writer John Joseph Mathews* with the University of Oklahoma Press in 2016. His creative writing has appeared in the book *Ain't Nobody That Can Sing Like Me: New Oklahoma Writing* (Ed. Jeanetta Calhoun Mish, Mongrel Empire Press), and in the journals *Sugar Mule, Red Truck Review, New Plains Review, Absolute,* and *Windmill,* among other places. A dozen of his scholarly articles have appeared in academic book collections or peer-reviewed journals. Snyder earned his PHD from the University of Oklahoma, his MA from the University of Colorado, and his BA from Haverford College. He is a Professor of English and Humanities at Oklahoma City Community College.

www.ingramcontent.com/pod-product-compliance
Lightning Source LLC
Chambersburg PA
CBHW071408170626
46811CB00003B/1308